Strategic Decision Making

Strategic Decision Making

A Best Practice Blueprint

GEORGE WRIGHT

JOHN WILEY & SONS, LTD

Chichester • New York • Weinheim • Brisbane • Singapore • Toronto

Copyright © 2001 by John Wiley & Sons, Ltd,
Baffins Lane, Chichester,
West Sussex PO19 1UD, England

National 01243 779777
International (+44) 1243 779777
e-mail (for orders and customer service enquiries):
cs-books@wiley.co.uk
Visit our Home Page on http://www.wiley.co.uk
or http://www.wiley.com

All Rights Reserved. No part of this publication may be reproduced, stored in a retrieval system, or transmitted, in any form or by any means, electronic, mechanical, photocopying, recording, scanning or otherwise, except under the terms of the Copyright, Designs and Patents Act 1988 or under the terms of a licence issued by the Copyright Licensing Agency, 90 Tottenham Court Road, London, W1P 9HE, UK, without the permission in writing of the publisher.

Other Wiley Editorial Offices

John Wiley & Sons, Inc., 605 Third Avenue,
New York, NY 10158-0012, USA

Wiley-VCH Verlag GmbH, Pappelallee 3,
D-69469 Weinheim, Germany

John Wiley & Sons Australia Ltd, 33 Park Road, Milton,
Queensland 4064, Australia

John Wiley & Sons (Asia) Pte Ltd, 2 Clementi Loop #02-01,
Jin Xing Distripark, Singapore 129809

John Wiley & Sons (Canada) Ltd, 22 Worcester Road,
Rexdale, Ontario M9W 1L1, Canada

British Library Cataloguing in Publication Data

A catalogue record for this book is available from the British Library

ISBN 0-471-48699-X

Typeset in 11/15pt ITC Garamond Light by Footnote Graphics, Warminster, Wiltshire
Printed and bound in Great Britain by Biddles Ltd, Guildford and King's Lynn.
This book is printed on acid-free paper responsibly manufactured from sustainable forestry, in which at least two trees are planted for each one used for paper production.

'The key resource of your organisation is the intellectual capability held in the heads of its managers. In many organisations, this resource is largely untapped. Unique competitive advantage lies in harnessing this intellectual capability and using it to drive your organisation forward.'

Contents

Series Foreword

I am delighted to be able to introduce to you the *CBI Fast Track Series*. The book you are holding is the outcome of a significant new publishing partnership between the CBI and John Wiley & Sons (Wiley). We intend it to be the first in a long line of high quality materials on which the CBI and Wiley collaborate. Before saying a little about this partnership, I would like to briefly introduce you to the CBI.

With a direct corporate membership employing over 4 million and a trade association membership representing over 6 million of the workforce, the CBI is the premier organisation speaking for companies in the UK. We represent directly and indirectly, over 200 000 companies employing more than 40% of the UK private sector workforce. The majority of blue-chip organisations and industry leaders from the FTSE 250 are members, as well as a significant number of small to medium sized companies (SMEs).* Our mission is to ensure that the government of the day, Whitehall, Brussels and the wider community understand the needs of British business. The CBI takes an active role in forming policies that enable UK companies to compete and prosper, and we ensure that the lines of communication between private and public leaders are always open on a national scale as well as via our regional networks.

The appropriateness of a link between the CBI and a leading business publisher like Wiley cannot be understated. Both organisations have a vested interest in efficiently and effectively serving the needs of businesses of all sizes. Both are forward-thinkers; constantly trend-spotting to envision where the next issues and concerns lie. Both maintain a global outlook in servicing the needs of its local customers. And finally, both champion the adoption of best practice amongst the groups they represent.

Which brings us back to this series. Each *CBI Fast Track* book offers a complete best practice briefing in a selected topic, along with a blueprint for successful implementation. The aim is to help enterprises achieve peak performance across key disciplines. The series will continue to evolve as new and different issues force their way to the top of the corporate agenda.

I do hope you enjoy this book and would encourage you to look out for further titles from the CBI and Wiley. Here's to all the opportunities the future holds and to *Fast Track* success with your own corporate agenda.

*Foreign companies that maintain registered offices in the UK are also eligible for CBI membership.

Digby Jones
Director-General, CBI

About the author

George Wright is a psychologist with knowledge of the way managers make decisions. His consultancy clients include IBM, ICL, Clerical Medical Investment Group, Philips, NEM Insurance, Thus, Stirling Council, Dumfries and Galloway Council, and Petronas. George's consultancy activities now focus on facilitating strategic thinking and scenario planning. In 1995 he was elected a Fellow of the Royal Society for the encouragement of Arts, Manufacturers and Commerce.

George is currently Professor and Deputy Director of the Graduate School of Business, and Principal of the Centre for Scenario Planning and Future Studies, based in the Graduate School of Business at Strathclyde University, Glasgow. Previously he held Faculty positions at London Business School and the University of Leeds Business School, and was recently a Visiting Professor at the Athens University of Economics and Business.

Founder and editor of the *Journal of Behavioral Decision Making* and on the editorial boards of the *Journal of Forecasting*, the *International Journal of Intelligent Systems in Accounting, Finance and Management* and *The Journal of Multi-Criteria Decision Analysis*, George has published widely. His books include *Judgmental Forecasting*, *Forecasting with Judgment* and *Decision Analysis for Management Judgment* (with Paul Goodwin), both published by Wiley, as well as two popular psychology titles published by Penguin Books.

Preface

This book answers several questions:

- Why are large organisations, like Marks & Spencer, sometimes accused of 'losing the plot' in their business strategy?
- Why did organisations like Electrolux, Miele and Bosch turn down the opportunity presented by Dyson's new vacuum cleaner design?
- Why was the Space Shuttle Challenger launched when it was clear to many insiders, at the time, that a major component would fail?
- Why did predictions of residential house price movements in the UK not anticipate the sharp rises and falls in the market over the last 15 years?
- Why were funds poured into the UK Millennium Dome and the City of London Taurus computer project when it was clear that 'good money' was following 'bad'?
- Why did Nick Leeson keep on trading covertly at Barings Bank in Singapore until his losses meant the bank would go bust?

The answers will surprise you. Using psychological theory, paper-and-pencil 'thought problems', and well-chosen quotations from newspaper articles written at the time, I will demonstrate and explain the causes of these 'strategic blunders'. I will also show you how to recognise and prevent your own organisation making the same mistakes. Having read this book you will:

- recognise that organisations avoid the stresses of confronting strategic dilemmas by delay, and by bolstering failing strategies;
- realise that a 'blame culture' within an organisation will lead to poor-quality decisions that are then likely, covertly, to escalate into even worse decisions for the organisation;

- be aware that managers' confidence in their ability to predict the future is often misplaced.

My prescriptions for improving strategic decision making include:

- use of frame analysis to help you reframe decisions and avoid strategic habits;
- use of dialectical inquiry and devil's advocacy techniques to promote dissenting opinions within top management teams and overcome 'group think';
- incorporation of scenario planning in your organisation's decision-making process in order to avoid overconfidence about the nature of the future.

In this book, I show that the key resource of your organisation is the intellectual capability held in the heads of its managers. In many organisations, this resource is largely untapped. Unique competitive advantage lies in harnessing this intellectual compatibility and using it to drive your organisation forward. This book explains how to make use of this resource, and illustrates what can happen to organisations that don't.

Acknowledgements

The idea for this book emerged when I was on a short appointment as a visiting professor at the Athens University of Economics and Business in 2000. During my stay, Gregory Prastacos allowed me time to think and plan the book. When I returned to Glasgow in April, Christine Reid helped me greatly by undertaking electronic searches through newspapers to locate articles on the activities of the organisations that I use to illustrate strategic blunders.

My thanks also to Maureen McDonald for giving priority to word-processing the many changes that the manuscript for this book went through.

ONE

Challenging Routines

In August 1972, Jay Brothers menswear was having problems in the recession. Sales were dropping off in most of its high-street shops, and even redoing the shopfronts and store layout had not had any noticeable impact. Jim Nott, managing director, pondered the issue. Their 200 shops meant strong purchasing power. For the last ten years they had sourced finished goods – casual menswear made to Jay Brothers' designs – from Hong Kong. But now, exchange rate changes had meant that supply costs were rising. Jim conferred with his purchasing director – Jay Brothers had to become more assertive with the suppliers in order to drive down costs, such that shop prices could be cut but profit margins maintained. For the first year, the strategy worked and sales figures improved, but then the figures worsened slightly.

Jim became more aggressive with Jay Brothers' suppliers, and again figures improved. The following year, Jim went on a tour of South-East Asian countries where labour rates and exchange rates were more favourable. Some excellent deals were struck. However, at the same time, new types of casual-wear stores were opening: Next, Gap, Principles for Men. Sales at Jay Brothers started to plummet. Jim took early retirement. Shortly afterwards, the Jay Brothers' name disappeared from the UK high streets.

What went wrong at Jay Brothers? Before we discuss this, try the following thought problem.

Thought problem 1

Imagine that you are given an 8-pint jug full of water, and a 5-pint jug and a 3-pint jug that are both empty. We will represent this as 8–8, 5–0 and 3–0, where the first figure indicates the size of the jug and the second figure indicates the amount of water in the jug. Your task is to pour the water from one jug into another until you end up with 6 pints in the 8-pint jug and 2 pints in the 3-pint jug (i.e. 8–6, 5–0, 3–2). Since the jugs are opaque, you can only tell if a jug is full, empty, or partly full.

What are the moves needed to change the initial state of the jugs into the goal state?

The easiest series of moves is as follows. It is worthwhile working through these moves:

	Jug 1	Jug 2	Jug 3
Initial state	8–8	5–0	3–0
Intermediate states	8–3	5–5	3–0
	8–3	5–2	3–3
	8–6	5–2	3–0
Goal state	8–6	5–0	3–2

First, jug 1 is used to fill jug 2. Then jug 2 is used to fill jug 3. Next, the contents of jug 3 are poured into jug 1, and finally, the contents of jug 2 are poured into jug 3. Do you follow this logic? Take your time and rework thought problem 1 until the steps to the solution are clear. When you have done this, try thought problem 2.

Thought problem 2

Imagine you have an 8-pint jug filled with water, an empty 5-pint jug and a 3-pint jug containing 1 pint of water (i.e. 8–8, 5–0, 3–1). The goal state is 8–6, 5–0, 3–3. Let us again follow the logic of the moves.

First, jug 1 is used to fill jug 2. Then jug 2 is used to fill jug 3. Next, jug 3 is poured into jug 1, and finally, the contents of jug 2 are poured into jug 3.

	Jug 1	Jug 2	Jug 3
Initial state	8–8	5–0	3–1
Intermediate states	8–3	5–5	3–1
	8–3	5–3	3–3
	8–6	5–3	3–0
Goal state	8–6	5–0	3–3

Do you follow the logic? Take your time and rework the steps in the solution. In fact, *should* you follow the logic? If you feel that you should, then think again! A more efficient solution to thought problem 2 would be simply to pour the contents of jug 1 into jug 3.

Success formulas

Psychologists have given individuals a series of problems to solve – like thought problem 1 – that can *only* be solved by a long sequence of moves that, over time, becomes a familiar 'success formula' to the individual problem solver. When the same people are eventually presented with a problem similar to thought problem 2, they try to follow the same 'success formula', rather than see the 'short cut'. By contrast, people who are simply presented with thought problem 2, without having experienced solving a sequence of problems like thought problem 1, see the straightforward solution without any difficulty. In other words, our thought processes tend to become *cognitive habits*, which, much like a machine, we use to solve problems in a predictable way.[1]

Jim Nott at Jay Brothers menswear also followed a 'success formula' that had always worked: expert procurement. But the world had changed in the late 1970s in the UK. Men had become more fashion conscious, and Jay Brothers' well-made, year-by-year cheaper, casual clothes were good buys but were simply no longer seen as stylish by more discerning men. Hence, Jay Brothers went out of business. Consider thought problem 3.

Thought problem 3

Below are nine dots. Your task is to draw four continuous straight lines, connecting all the dots, without lifting your pencil from the paper. The correct solution is shown in Appendix A. Try the problem first, and then refer to the solution.

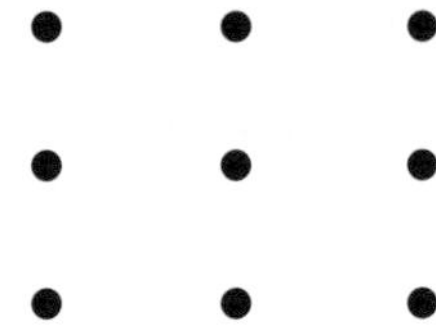

Did you have difficulty solving the nine-dot problem? If so, you are like most of those I have given the problem to in my MBA and executive classes. Assumptions made about problems are called 'frames', or ways of seeing.

Frames of reference

In organisations, the roles that people occupy can influence the way that problems are seen or framed. For example, a cosmetic products company was losing money in the early 1980s. Key managers in the company were asked to investigate and report on the reasons for the decline. The marketing managers thought that the cause of the problem was lack of advertising and promotional support. The manufacturing and distribution managers blamed inaccurate sales forecasting and lack of customer knowledge on the part of the marketing group, while the finance department blamed budget overruns by all departments. Finally, the legal department identified that a lack of new franchising and licensing agreements meant that the company lacked new products to sell.[2]

It is clear that poor framing may mean that managers set out to solve the wrong problem because they have created a framework for a decision with little thought. The best options may be overlooked. Well-rehearsed and familiar ways of making decisions will be dominant and difficult to change – just as with Jay Brothers menswear.

In large and successful organisations, current ways of doing business will become embedded more and more deeply as the years pass. For example, consider the majority of companies within the UK and US auto industries in the late 1970s. The focus was on manufacturing long production runs with minimum redesigns. By contrast, other countries' manufacturing frames were more customer oriented, in that responsiveness to changes in customer demand was the focus. In the UK and the USA, the high level of commitment to a – previously successful – production-oriented strategy meant that management was slow to adapt to a world where changes in customer preferences mean that past demand is no longer predictive of future demand. In some companies, attention to the changing desires of customers can be limited. A marketing focus is not necessarily a universal characteristic of companies that have been in business for many years. Consider the following abstracts from articles about Marks & Spencer, a major UK clothing retailer. I have chosen those aspects of the articles that relate to Marks & Spencer's framing of the way to do business as a clothing and speciality food retailer.

'Tattered and torn by plunging profits, Marks & Spencer is trying to win back our loyalty' by John Walsh, *Independent* 7 November 1999 (Copyright 1999 Newspaper Publishing Plc)

The old dame kicking over the traces! Is that how Britain's largest retailer wants to be seen from now on? If the marketing department is to be believed, everything is going to change. The in-store design, untouched in what seems like decades, will be rethought ...

More crucially, the clothes will be different, and the way they are marketed. Because, after years of a caution that has sometimes seemed to border on paranoia, M&S is diving into the churning surf of fashion trendiness ... For the first time, it will capitalise on the names of the designers behind the St

Michael label. There's talk of M&S catwalk shows in the autumn. There's even talk, for the first time ever, of a TV advertising campaign.

If all this image-burnishing suggests a company in the throes of a shuddering nervous breakdown, you can hardly blame them. For M&S has just survived the most horrendous year in its history ... 'In 45 years of retailing,' said the recently retired chairman, Sir Richard Greenbury, 'I've never seen the figures go from good to bad so quickly.' The new chief executive Peter Salsbury laid off 290 store management staff on 11 May, having already removed 200 buyers at head office and 31 senior executives. The blood-letting allegedly saved £10m – but what was that compared with the millions the chain was losing from customer disaffection? The awful fact was plain: the British buying public had ceased to love Marks and Sparks.

For years the nation and the store chain had a relationship like no other. In the sixties, M&S transcended its status as a shop and became iconic; it stood for a certain stodgy brand of eccentric British decency, like the Albert Memorial, the Proms or the Queen Mother. To criticise M&S for being old-fashioned was pointless. It was the nation's secret necessity, the underwear drawer of the realm. It still is. British women buy their knickers at M&S at a rate of a million a week ... But as the high street clothes shops became increasingly sophisticated, and signed up premier-league designers to create 'diffusion ranges' of their catwalk triumphs – Jasper Conran at Debenhams, Hussein Chalayan at Top Shop and Liza Bruce at Dorothy Perkins – M&S refused to join in ... Shoppers grew disenchanted with the range ...

It was on that assumption of quality that the company traded for far too long. The shop interiors stayed blank and off-putting. The in-store signs and labels became increasingly curt and unseductive. 'Cotton' one sign would announce in front of a display of 200 shirts ... The company never advertised on TV or in the newspapers. Only lately was the concept of putting changing rooms in more than its flagship shops taken up; it assumed that, if you could bring it back and change it, why bother trying it on? ...

How did the designers feel? Brian Godbold, former design director of M&S, now a consultant, describes the frustration of the creative marketeer. 'When I joined the company, 20 years ago, the prevailing wisdom among senior management was: "Good goods sell arse-upwards". It thought that if the merchandise was good enough, it would sell anyway. My designer friends in those days, like Ossie Clark and Bill Gibb, said "You're mad to go near a chain store"; but what's happened to chain stores in the past two decades has been phenomenal.'

Godbold is buoyant about the new management. 'Peter Salsbury's management style couldn't be more different from Sir Richard Greenbury's,' he said. 'Ideas are allowed to come up through the system, decisions are taken in a much more open way. There's a big change in the way people work. It's accepted that, even if you have a good product, you must have other things too. We didn't realise how important service and interior design are to the package. We recognise it now; we're back on track and feel positive about the future.'

... But one can only marvel at this creaking old dowager of the retail aristocracy, as she takes her first faltering steps, on her zebra-print evening shoes, into the world of marketing, advertising, interior design and perceived value. She would do almost anything to have us love her again. Will she succeed?

'Every mistake that could be made. Marks & Spencer came to Canada thinking it was just like home and never quite recovered' by Marina Strauss, *Globe and Mail Metro* 6 July 1999 (Copyright 1999 Thomson Canada Ltd)

Cope and Constance Schwenger were in a mood to stock up when they headed off to Marks & Spencer's Canadian flagship store in the Holt Renfrew Centre on Toronto's posh Bloor Street West.

They were after their favourite cheese biscuits.

Unfortunately, the cheese biscuits were sold out, but the couple didn't leave empty-handed. They picked up two packages of digestive cookies – $2.59 each. This is not the kind of business that Marks & Spencer had in mind when it set up shop in the exclusive shopping district three years ago. After a quarter-century in the Canadian marketplace and just three profitable years, it needed customers willing to spring for much more than the occasional box of crackers …

… What went wrong?

'I think everybody in the UK who had anything to do with it would say every mistake that could possibly have been made was made,' said company president David Stewart…

How one of Britain's leading retailers allowed this to happen began as a lesson in marketing arrogance, according to John Torella, a retail consultant who once dealt with the chain.

'They just figured, "We don't need to advertise, everybody knows us. People are just going to come and find out about us."'

Michael Waitzer, a former Marks & Spencer executive and now a vice-president with Tip Top Tailors, agreed. 'The typical British philosophy was: It works here, so it should work in Canada.'

Feeling no need to advertise wasn't the company's only failure to connect with Canadian tastes. For example, it assumed that shoppers would be aware of the perfect Marks & Spencer fit, so the stores had no changing rooms to let them try garments on. Clive Nickolds, who was company president in the early nineties, said he quickly realized that the similarities between Canada and Britain 'can be much overstated'.

'When we first started, we underestimated the differences,' recalled the 32-year Marks & Spencer veteran, now in London as head of the European division. 'We plunked down a British formula in a foreign country. We thought that because most people spoke English and most people were expatriates – which was complete nonsense, of course – we could just put the formula down without any adaptation and it would sell as well as it did in the UK

'It took us rather a long time to realize that wasn't the case'…

There were certainly attempts made to turn things around. In time, the changing rooms appeared, although the attitude toward advertising remained inconsistent. Mr Torella remembers developing a high-profile campaign in the early 1990s to promote the new, more contemporary-looking stores and fashions that the chain had embraced. At the last minute, London head office killed the $250,000 blitz, opting for a cheaper, more traditional pitch ...

'They've got the world's greatest biscuits, and I am going to miss them,' Mr Schwenger said, conceding that 'we haven't bought the things they want us to buy.'

Sheila McEachen, 34, has been another regular shopper, mainly just for the high-quality underwear. 'The styles are kind of maternal, targeted to older women,' said the 34-year-old public relations manager. 'For the longest time it was your mother's store. They were trying to break out of that. They've changed over the years .... It was just too late'...

According to Mrs Schwenger, the final blow did not come as a complete surprise.

'When Marks & Spencer moved onto Bloor Street, I kept looking in the window and thinking, they're just not making it. They just didn't have the zip to their styling that would entice people to come.'

For example, when she goes clothes shopping for her children, the Gap gets the nod. 'It's more cutting edge.'

It is clear that an organisation may decline or go out of business if its managers fail to change their business frame so that it is more closely in tune with changes in the world.[3] For example, consider in the late 1970s a manufacturer of watches whose expertise is in producing accurate, miniaturised, clockwork movements. This company's competencies in clockwork will, of course, turn out to be ill-matching to the extreme accuracy and cheapness of quartz watch technology in the mid-1980s. Consider also the manufacturers of bowler hats, solid rubber car tyres, valve radios and valve televisions. Each of these manufacturers would have developed capabilities/competencies – perhaps unique ones – in their manufacturing/development processes. The problem is, of course, that valued competencies may become irrelevant as changes in technology or fashion sense occur. The key to success is not to be tied too closely to current ways of doing business or 'success formulas'. Success formulas and tried-and-trusted approaches should be open to challenge, debate and dissent. Consider the following article about Robert Dyson's attempt to interest well-established vacuum cleaner manufacturers in his new design of vacuum cleaner.

'Interview: Lucky sucker James Dyson revolutionised the vacuum cleaner and has "sucked up" a £500 million fortune.' by Daire O'Brien, 19 December 1999, *Sunday Business Post* (Copyright © 1999 *Sunday Business Post*; Source: World Reporter (TM))

In 1979, Dyson found out that the standard vacuum cleaner, or the hoover, as it was generically known on this side of the Atlantic, was far from where it could have been. The suction ability of the machine tailed off miserably when its bag was only 10 per cent full, as the dust clogged the air outlet. He also sensed that the market was dormant, dominated by companies like Hoover and Electrolux that had never had to face a serious bit of competition in their life.

He invented a bagless vacuum cleaner that kept its suction power at 100 per cent, thanks to a design breakthrough known as the dual cyclone. The 'hoover without the bag' was treated much like a plane without wings. People had trouble accepting that it could work.

'I went to Electrolux twice. I went to Miele. I went to Bosch and all the others. They all had a good look at it, but no-one would sign up,' he recalls. 'I didn't get the impression they were that interested in change. They are now, of course, but that's because it's been forced on them.'

Risk taking versus risk aversion

Now let's move on to another demonstration of framing effects on decision making. Thought problem 4 asks you to make a policy decision.[4]

Thought problem 4

Imagine that the USA is preparing for the outbreak of an unusual viral disease, which is expected to kill 600 people. Two alternative programmes to combat the disease have been proposed. Assume that the exact scientific estimate of the consequences of the programs are as follows: If programme A is adopted, 200 will be saved. If programme B is adopted, there is a 1:3 probability that 600 people will be saved, and a 2:3 probability that no people will be saved. If you had to make the choice, which of the two programmes would you favour?

Well, if you are like most people then you tend to favour programme A. Such a choice is risk averse, in that the prospect of certainly saving 200 lives is more attractive than a risky prospect of equal expected value. By 'expected value', we mean the probability of our outcome multiplied by the value of that outcome. For programme A, the expected value is a 100% chance of 200 lives saved, whereas in programme B the expected value is $1/3 \times 600$ plus $2/3 \times 0 = 200$. So, both programme A and programme B have an equivalent expected value of 200. However, imagine if instead you had been presented with the same cover story but with a different statement of the outcomes of the alternative programmes as follows: If programme C is adopted, 400 people will die. If programme D is adopted, there is a 1:3 probability that nobody will die, and a 2:3 probability that 600 people will die.

In this formulation, most respondents favour programme D. This option is *risk taking* in that the certain death of 400 people is less acceptable than the two-in-three chance that 600 will die. Choices involving gains (e.g. between programmes A and B) are often risk averse, and choices involving losses (e.g. between programmes C and D) are often risk taking. Notice that the choice between A and B is identical to the choice between C and D. The only difference is that the first choice emphasises lives saved, while the second choice emphasises lives lost. This simple change of frame produces a dramatic shift in choice.

Multiple frames

Without realising it, we tend to see reality through one frame at a time, and once locked into a frame, it is difficult to switch frames. Even physicians – who might be expected to know how to think dispassionately about life and death – are influenced inappropriately by the reference point, in this case lives saved versus lives lost, in problems similar to the one above.[5] Ideally, decision problems should be examined through more than one frame of reference.

Imagine a business in difficulty that is facing a choice between two options – both of which carry the risk of losses. The tendency will be to favour the option that *may* deliver the better pay off, even if it is the riskier option. By contrast, in more comfortable times, the business will tend to choose options that are risk averse. The former risk-taking orientation in the domain of losses is illustrated well by the events in the downfall of Nick Leeson as he tried to recover from his gradually deteriorating final position as a futures trader. We shall have more to say about Nick Leeson in Chapter 6. As an example of risk-averse choices in times of abundance, imagine that you are in a well-paid, secure and interesting job. If someone offered you another job, you would have to be 100% sure that the alternative job was better before you would seriously consider a job change.

An identical choice problem can be framed differently – as a choice involving gains, or as a choice involving losses – and, depending on this framing, your favoured choice will be different. The key to improved decision making, then, is to seek out different framings of the same strategic situation, because the frame that you adopt will influence the choice that you make.

Using frame analysis

How can this be achieved? One response is to make use of 'frame analysis', a set of simple questions that you pose to yourself or your management team.[6] The six key questions to ask are:

1. What aspects of the situation are downplayed?
2. What reference points are used to measure success?
3. What does the frame emphasise?

4. What does it minimise?
5. Do others in the same industry segment think about the issue differently?
6. Is the decision one involving potential gains or one involving potential losses?

In terms of Jim Nott and Jay Brothers' menswear, the answers to these six questions are straightforward:

1. Causes of poor sales other than price.
2. (i) Sourcing finished goods at cheaper prices.
   (ii) Year-on-year sales figures that are, at least, constant.
3. Becoming more aggressive/resourceful in sourcing finished goods.
4. Market/customer orientation.
5. Yes, others sell multiple brands (other than own brands) of casual wear.
6. The decision is one prompted by current losses.

By completing a frame analysis you will, as a result, put alternative framings of a strategic issue onto the agenda of the management team. As we shall see in later chapters, we advocate several other methods to ensure that the management team will consider carefully these new agenda items and thus overcome framing bias. All the methods that we advocate focus on enabling the management team to challenge current ways of doing business. As stated in the subtitle to this book, we believe that the most precious asset of any organisation is the intellectual resource residing in the minds of its management team. Methods that can bring this resource to bear, in order to challenge current ways of thinking, have the potential to pay out massive dividends to the organisation. But, as we shall also see in the next chapter, it is commonplace that individual managers find it difficult, if not impossible, to challenge 'success formulas'. Often, no-one speaks out as an organisation sinks into decline. In our view, the key task of top management is to encourage challenge and debate, and hence harness the intellectual resources of the management team. As we shall see, a similar-thinking management team who seldom debate issues is, in itself, a tell-tale sign of an organisation that may not be able to adapt early enough to change.

Key messages

Challenge the routine. Challenge success formulas. Recognise that choices involving gains are often risk averse, and that choices involving losses are often risk seeking. Make use of frame analysis to generate alternative viewpoints and overcome framing bias. Remember that organisational decline is often a direct result of complacency in top management teams.

Our examples of outdated recipes for success at Marks and Spencer and Robert Dyson's failed attempts to interest Bosch, Miele and Electrolux in his new vacuum cleaner design illustrate that managers' framing of ways to do business can become embedded more and more deeply in successful organisations as the years pass. But such recipes for success will, eventually, become less well matched to the business environment. Challenging complacency by challenging framing holds the key to ensuring your organisation's continuing success.

TWO

Decision Making in Management Teams

The meeting started, and Jim Bolt the chief executive spoke. He outlined his position on the threats facing the business. Although competition was getting fiercer, the firm had strengths that had been built up over the years. New products had been introduced and these would surely be successful. The last prototype had been ready on time and had performed well in the factory tests. The prototype was built with the unique competencies of Beta Co. and Jim estimated that the firm had a two-year lead over rival products. Jim looked around his management team. They all nodded in agreement. Jim was not surprised at their agreement with his evaluation of Beta Co.'s situation. He had been through the logic very carefully and, to stay ahead, Beta Co. had to be R&D led. There really was no choice. One of the management team did look less than happy, though. John Pearman said that he was unsure whether further investment in the quartz-based technology was the best way forward. He had heard that competitor companies were investing differently. John spoke for a short while on this, but quickly gave way to the groundswell of support for Jim. Jim asked again, 'Are we all agreed?' Everyone nodded. John Pearman nodded and looked at the carpet. So, it was settled. The management team planned for large-scale production of the essential prototype design. All aspects of this were thought through in detail. Nothing was left to chance. Six months later, some press reports suggested that Westex Co. were about to launch an innovative alternative to Beta Co.'s new model. A photocopy of one of the press cuttings found its way onto Jim's desk. He read it and put it to one side. Next, he phoned the production department. The new machines were on order and would be delivered soon. Everything was in place.

Did Jim Bolt handle the decision process wisely? Notice that Jim outlined his position first. He holds the role of chief executive, so it is fair to say that he will be listened to by his subordinates. John Pearman raised a dissenting voice, but he soon quietened and went along with the majority of the 'yes-sayers'. No real effort was made by anyone to find out more about the technology other companies were investing in. Much later, press reports – which may have provided more information on competitor activity – were put to one side. In short, a decision once made is seldom reversed.

The next quotation illustrates the point. It is taken from an article in the magazine *Newsweek*, which was published on 28 January 1991. The article was written by a journalist who was analysing the reasons for US unpreparedness for Saddam Hussein's invasion of Kuwait:

> In the days leading up to the invasion, the intelligence agencies sent President Bush a list of predictions. The list was arranged in order of probability. 'None had as their first choice the prediction that Saddam Hussein would attack,' says one intelligence operative who saw the reports. Prediction No 1 was that Saddam was bluffing. Prediction No 2 was that he might seize part of the Rumaila oilfield that straddles Iraq and Kuwait and possibly Warba and Bubiyan islands, two mudflats blocking Iraq's access to the Persian Gulf. It was assumed that he would pull back from Kuwait once the islands were secured. 'The line we kept hearing around here was that he has just massed there along the Kuwait border to drive up the price of oil,' recalls one senior Pentagon officer. 'If people were saying he is for real and he is going to invade, it was not briefed to us as definite.'
>
> Several sounder voices did predict an invasion but they went unheard. One midlevel Mideast analyst at the CIA got it right, but his warning 'got lost' in the momentum of the opposing consensus. Marine Corps Officers, scanning satellite photos that showed Iraqi air-defence units, tanks and artillery deployed forward at the Kuwait border, surmised that this could only mean an invasion, but they kept their silence because of bureaucratic pressures. The Defence Intelligence Agency's top analyst for the Middle East was convinced that Saddam would invade and

warned the Senate Intelligence Committee that the dictator might not be bluffing. His own shop did not buy it. The DIA went along with the pack.

While the Iraqis and the Kuwaitis gathered in Jeddah for a final haggle over oil and borders, the House Foreign Affairs Committee summoned John Kelly, the assistant secretary of state covering the Mideast, to explain what was going on. 'If Iraq for example charged into Kuwait for whatever reason, what would our position be with regard to the use of US forces?' chairman Lee Hamilton inquired. 'That, Mr Chairman, is a hypothetical or a contingency question, the kind which I cannot get into,' Kelly replied.

From this journalistic analysis, three major points emerge. The first is that consideration was devoted only to those events seen as most likely. The second is that once the group of decision makers had made up its mind as to what was going to happen, even conclusive information that the prediction (decision) was poor did not change the prediction. Those individuals who expressed dissenting opinion soon quelled their dissent and went along with the pack. Given such (inappropriate) confidence in the prediction of Saddam Hussein's intent, then contingency planning for events seen as low probability was minimal or even zero.

Groupthink

This tendency of management teams to concur is an illustration of 'groupthink'.[1] Management teams are often made up by people with homogeneous backgrounds: university degree holders, middle-class people, nationals of the country where the organisation is based, etc. Also, many will have families, mortgages and career paths, so to speak out may risk one's job. In high-consequence situations – such as in major investment decisions or discussions of strategic direction – the likelihood of dissenting voices being raised after the most senior person has stated their opinion is small. The likelihood of continuing dissent (at least overtly) is even smaller. Irving Janis has remarked:

> *In my earlier research with ordinary citizens I had been impressed by the effects – both unfavourable and favourable – of the social pressures that develop in cohesive groups ... Members tend to evolve informal objectives to reserve friendly intergroup relations, and this becomes part of the hidden agenda at meetings ... ordinary citizens become more concerned with retaining the approval of fellow members of their work group than with coming up with good solutions to the task in hand.*

Groupthink is essentially the suppression by the group (or management team) of ideas that are critical of the direction in which the group is moving. It is reflected in a tendency to concur with the position and views that are perceived as favoured by the group. Such cohesive groups tend to develop rationalisations for the invulnerability of the group's decision or strategy, and inhibit the expression of critical ideas by dissenting members of the management team. Consider the following articles that document the suppression of dissenting viewpoints at Marks & Spencer and at NASA. In the latter case, the decison-making failures that led to the disastrous launch of the space shuttle Challenger were analysed by an investigatory commission; the Commission's findings are reported across the latter three articles.

'Losing the way down Baker Street at Marks & Spencer HQ: as profits plummet, no-one dares say the "S" word to the chairman' by Kate Rankin, the *Daily Telegraph*, 11 July 1998 (Copyright 1998 The *Telegraph* plc, London)

Take a bus down Oxford Street, late on a weekday afternoon. The Christmas decorations are appearing in the windows, prompting the reassuring ritual groans that it's getting earlier every year, and those stores which are not already overwhelmed with tinsel have sparkly party frocks to cheer up the passers-by.

Then you come to Marks & Spencer's flagship store at Marble Arch. 'Great autumn value' some rather grim orange posters say, as if to reinforce the suspicion that M&S, Britain's premier retailer, has lost the plot.

Suddenly, the giant looks leaden and dowdy. This week it has announced a 23pc fall in first-half profits ... As the market digested the numbers, M&S shares tumbled to their lowest level for more than three years as everyone wondered whether something had gone dreadfully wrong at this much-loved British high street institution ...

Even for its fans, dear old M&S is looking a bit dull when compared to the big-name designers at Debenhams, which include Jasper Conran, Ben de Lisi and Pearce Fionda. As for the home furnishings at M&S, it looks almost old-fashioned when compared to Debenhams' newly-launched range from the designer Kelly Hoppen ...

Boots's presentation, two days after the M&S results, showed how it can target individual shoppers, cosseting them and drawing them back to the stores. Analysts were so impressed that they ignored the indifferent trading numbers and the shares shot up by a tenth.

M&S, by contrast, does not even have a loyalty card, and seems in danger of missing out the information revolution.

Part of the reason, analysts suspect, is the inward-looking culture of the company. For all its size, its executives are nearly all home-grown (and it is curious how poorly many of them do if they are head-hunted to other retailers).

This culture is reinforced by the mentality of Greenbury. For the chairman of a company with sales more than £8 billion, Greenbury, 62, is extraordinarily sensitive to anything he regards as criticism ...

'The only things that matter to him are his family, Manchester United and M&S. He is passionate about M&S. It's his life. That's the reason he is so sensitive and takes any criticism to heart,' the director said.

Analysts and journalists who write about M&S in terms he dislikes receive lengthy letters, headed 'from Sir Richard Greenbury', in response. His infamous letters rarely come on M&S

writing paper and have been dubbed 'Rickograms' in the City. Some analysts even collect them …

Those who really upset him may be summoned round to Baker Street for a telling-off over lunch … Greenbury, whose sheer size (he's 6ft 2in) can be intimidating, insists: 'I'm not an ogre. I'm blunt and I'm competitive.' The hordes of silent M&S identikits attending Tuesday's press conference seemed terrified of him.

But what makes him really cross is the thorny issue of succession. 'Please, don't mention the "S" word,' his underlings plead. 'The chairman is not in a very good mood' …

One analyst, who insists on remaining anonymous for fear of yet another Rickogram, says: 'It must be extremely difficult running M&S when the managing directors are manoeuvring for the chief executive's job. No-one knows who is going to be running the company in two or three years' time, so it must be difficult to plan for the future.'

'NASA's decisions questioned. Shuttle pre-launch process "may have been flawed"' by Storer Rowley, *Chicago Tribune*, 16 February 1986 (Copyright *Chicago Tribune* 1986)

The chairman of the presidential commission investigating the space shuttle Challenger explosion said Saturday that NASA's decision-making process leading up to the shuttle launch 'may have been flawed'…

Commission members were reportedly deeply concerned by the assessment of astronaut Robert Crippen, who has flown on five shuttle missions and is now deputy director of flight crew operations for the shuttle program, that the space agency seemed to change its usual pattern of launch decisions with the Challenger mission.

Crippen reportedly told the commission behind closed doors during a two-day visit last week to the Kennedy Space Center near Cape Canaveral, Fla.: 'Ever since I came to the manned space program, NASA's approach has been: "Prove this craft is ready to fly." It seems that in the case of this launch, the approach was: "Prove to me it isn't ready to fly." If that was the case, it was a serious mistake'...

At least two witnesses from Morton Thiokol Inc., the Chicago-based company that manufactured the solid fuel booster rocket which investigators are focusing on as a possible cause of the Challenger catastrophe, told the commission during closed sessions at the Cape that they recommended to their superiors against launching the shuttle ...

One source familiar with the commission's investigation said there is concern among commission members about whether those who evaluated the flightworthiness of the craft had reservations about launching Challenger and whether such reservations were given appropriate attention.

The source, who asked not to be identified, said commission members were trying to determine whether those concerns were passed along to NASA officials on high enough levels, and 'whether they were heeded to the extent that they should have been.'

Specifically, he noted, some officials had reservations concerning the subfreezing temperatures before launch and the launch temperature of 38 degrees, a record low for all 25 shuttle missions so far. There were concerns about possible effects of the cold on Challenger's sensitive solid rocket fuel and on rubber seals called O-rings that are used in booster field joints to prevent hot gases from leaking out ...

The commission members 'became particularly concerned about the decision-making process after two days at Kennedy,' the source said. They were concerned that there were 'a number of signposts along the road' indicating that it might have been unwise to proceed with the Challenger launch, particularly questions about 'key things', including booster 'seals and the O-rings'.

Asked if there were flaws in NASA's communications process, the source said. 'One could make that assumption. It all comes down to who raised red flags? At what stage? Why? Who saw those red flags? Why and what did they do about it when they saw them?'

'That's really what this (Rogers) statement issue boils down to,' the source said. 'Somebody warned and said, "This is not quite ready to go." Who did they tell? What did that person tell?

How far up the line did that go, and what was the reaction on the part of the people who received the concerns and apprehension? The implied concerns are on the O-rings and that it didn't reach a high enough level.'

Asked if commission members felt there was a cover-up by NASA, the source quickly said, 'Oh, no. No, not by any means. What happened is maybe people raised concerns about flight readiness. And maybe someone said, "We see, but it's not as bad or as risky as you think"'…

'Were the concerns of sufficient gravity to be taken up the line?' is the key question, the source said. 'A cover-up is not it at all.'

The source said there may have been an 'institutional problem' among longtime NASA officials, who 'may have not felt they had to tell' their superiors about 'red flags' raised on the day of launch and before.

'It is a case of technical experts issuing warnings which obviously didn't get the attention they deserved,' said the source. 'There are different levels of NASA. I don't say there's a cover-up, just that the system is flawed.'

'NASA aides deny decision was "flawed"' by Storer Rowley, *Chicago Tribune* (contributing to this story were Hanke Gratteau in Chicago, Michael Tackett in Washington, and Howard Witt in Houston), 1 March 1986 (Copyright *Chicago Tribune* 1986)

…'In my judgment, the process was not flawed,' declared William Lucas, director of the Marshall Space Flight Center. Lucas and four other top shuttle managers … repeated their testimony, given over three days of public hearings in Washington before the Rogers panel, that they had been unaware Morton Thiokol engineers continued to unanimously oppose the launch even after company management overruled them.

The Morton Thiokol engineers said they feared the record cold would cause rubber seals in the seams of the booster rocket to fail. After lengthy telephone conferences on the night of Jan. 27 between NASA and Morton Thiokol just hours before the launch, company executives overruled their engineers to approve the launch, testimony showed.

In Houston, NASA official Jesse Moore, who gave the final order to launch the shuttle, said he is not ready to agree that NASA's decision-making process is flawed.

'I'm not throwing in the towel and saying the process is bad. I'm not prepared to make any judgments on changing the process. We all believe the process is a good process,' Moore told reporters. Moore took over Friday as the director of the Johnson Space Center in Houston. A source familiar with the presidential commission investigating the Challenger disaster said commission members 'expressed surprise at Marshall's comments, saying it was curious . . . in light of the facts. And that kind of comment underscores what is clearly a fundamental problem with the decision-making process.'

... Lucas said ... 'Let me say that I don't know that the [Morton Thiokol] executives saw them, either, but someone saw those memos and should have not stopped the memo that suggested there was a safety problem without passing it on.'

Engineers for Morton Thiokol testified this week that they opposed launch because they feared the cold would inhibit the O-rings from expanding to fill the crucial gap in the rocket seams ... But Lucas declared that, based on what his subordinates have told him, 'I think it was a sound decision to launch. So far as I know . . . my people did not know of the feelings of certain Thiokol engineers that have been expressed in recent days to the commission'...

'Commission finds flaws in NASA decision-making' (Challenger investigations) by R. Jeffrey Smith, *Science* 1237, 14 March 1986 (Copyright 1986 American Association for the Advancement of Science)

Commission finds Flaws in NASA Decision-making

In the last hours before the ill-fated launch of the space shuttle Challenger, senior officials of the National Aeronautics and Space Administration (NASA) were gathered in a corner of the launch control center to supervise final preparations. Four of them knew of a highly contentious discussion the previous evening about the effect of low temperatures on the performance of the shuttle's booster rockets, and of a unanimous initial recommendation by Morton Thiokol, Inc. that the launch be postponed because some rocket seals might fail.-1

But none of the four – who were directly responsible for the booster program's success or failure – thought to inform the others in the control room of Thiokol's anxieties. As a result, Jesse Moore, Arnold Aledrich, and Gene Thomas, the three principal agency officials empowered to arrest a launch and to rejuggle the shuttle's schedule, were kept in the dark about a problem that could, and apparently did, lead to a catastrophic accident and a lengthy setback for the manned space program …

The vigor with which NASA criticized Thiokol's observations that night has been a topic of considerable discussion. Lund, McDonald, Boisjoly, and two others from Thiokol testified that they felt considerable pressure from negative comments by Larry Mulloy, Marshall's booster program director, who 6 months earlier had told his superiors in Washington that he considered the seal problem 'closed'. Additionally pressure was felt from a remark by Hardy that he was 'appalled' by the initial Thiokol recommendation, and from repeated requests that Thiokol's managers offer their own opinion about the risks of seal failure.

Hardy explained that he is always 'likely to probe and sometimes even challenge either a pro position or a con position. The objective of this is just simply to test the data, test the degree of understanding . . . . I think anybody that knows me would realize that that is not interpreted as coming on strong or applying pressure.' Similar explanations were offered by Mulloy, but commission chairman Rogers did not buy them. Noting that NASA had recently invited other firms to compete for Thiokol's contract, he noted that 'they were under a lot of commercial pressure to give you the answer you wanted. And they construed what you and Mr. Hardy said to mean that you wanted them to change their minds.'…

Of course, nothing seems as clear-cut before a mistake as afterward. But the commission at present is showing little patience for the space agency's arguments.

Groupthink will result in a failure to examine – in any thorough way – the risks of the preferred strategy and a failure to work out contingency plans if the preferred course of action fails. A high level of group cohesiveness and a high level of external threat are characteristic of groupthink. In the case of the Challenger launch decision, a non-launch would have threatened public support for what had been promoted as a standard, day-to-day operational activity.

Alleviating groupthink

How can groupthink tendencies in management teams be alleviated? The key lies in the hands of the leader of the organisation. To overcome groupthink the leader should:

- withhold his or her own ideas at first;
- encourage new ideas and criticisms;
- make sure that the group listens to minority views;
- use processes designed to delay the management team forming an early consensus.

Remember, a decision – once made – is seldom reversed.

Two systematic methods for formalising dissension and debate within the organisation are the methods of dialectical inquiry (DI) and devil's advocacy.[2] Both require commitment from the top of the organisation.

Dialectical inquiry

There are three steps to this method:

1. Divide the management team into two: team A and team B. Team A prepares its position on the issue of concern, and then presents this verbally to team B.
2. Team B prepares a position that is deliberately designed to be an alternative to that proposed by team A, and then presents this to team A.
3. Teams A and B come together to debate their assumptions and recommendations.

Devil's advocacy

1. Divide the management team into two: team C prepares and then presents its position on the issue of concern to team D.
2. Team D prepares and presents a critique of team A's position, carefully probing all the elements of the position and recommendations.
3. Teams C and D come together to debate their assumptions and recommendations.

Both the DI and DA techniques encourage subgroups in the management team to generate a wide range of alternative strategies/courses of action. The techniques minimise any tendency to premature agreement or too-early closure on a single way forward. The processes lead, necessarily, to a more critical evaluation of assumptions, and provide a formal method for encouraging dissenting opinion. The end result is that the management team will reach a higher level of understanding of the rationale and strengths/weaknesses of the finally agreed decision. However, the two techniques are not without difficulties. A key concern is that the individuals in the management team maintain a focus on the facts surrounding the decision. Without this focus, personalities may become a focus of discussion. A key, also, is that the participants should avoid a win–lose approach to the debate. Remember, this is simply a role-playing exercise of dissension in order to provide a full exploration of strategic options. The dissension that is necessarily encouraged by the process is useful and positive, in that old ideas will be scrutinised closely and new ideas will have airtime. Some participants will, naturally, use humour to relieve the interpersonal tensions that can build as the debate becomes real.

At step 3 in both the DI and the DA method, the debate must be drawn to an end. A decision must, of course, eventually be made! Most participants will leave happily if they feel that their individual views have been heard by the group. The leader should summarise the positions that have emerged during the process before calling the question and moving the decision forward. In general, DA and DI are most useful for complex, ill-structured, strategic choices rather than more structured, routine decisions where the options and potential outcomes are reasonably clear-cut. However, both methods may result in ideas and directions that challenge or counter the leader's preferred position. In order to accept such challenges, the leader must be prepared to defer to the ideas of others. For Jim Bolt, discussed in the short case that initiated this chapter, this would perhaps not be easy. For John Pearman, the airtime that the methods would give him would, perhaps, be grasped eagerly. We will return to describe other methods to harness the intellectual resource of the organisation in Chapter 8.

Key messages

Recognise the pitfalls of groupthink. Give airtime to minority viewpoints. Delay early consensus seeking in decision making. Encourage dissension and debate in management teams, since early consensus and strong cohesion in top teams indicate poor decision making. Remember, a decision once taken is seldom reversed.

Our examples from Marks & Spencer's style of management and NASA's disastrous launch of the space shuttle Challenger illustrate the negative impact that decision-making processes can have when they act to suppress dissenting viewpoints. The methods of dialectical inquiry and devil's advocacy provide structures for encouraging the critical evaluation of proposed decisions, such that there is a higher level of understanding of the rationale and strengths/weaknesses of the finally agreed decision.

THREE

Overcoming Overconfidence

Joe Blott considered the future for Graham Pharmaceuticals. Everything hinged on the success of the new prototype drug, Clodene. Joe's best guess was that the drug would be ready for market within two years. Or, at least he felt 90% sure of this. He felt 100% sure that the drug would be ready within a three-year time horizon. His industry contacts were excellent, and he felt sure that no other company was working on a prototype with similar characteristics. Graham Pharmaceutical's new drug would be a world leader. The current animal tests had produced staggering results. The future looked assured. He was confident in his judgement. He had been in the business for 30 years – he couldn't recall being far out with his judgement before.

How good is Joe's judgement of the future? Let's consider this issue shortly. First, complete thought problem 5.[1]

Thought problem 5

For each of the ten quantities listed below, (i) write down your best estimate of that quantity and (ii) put a lower and upper bound around your estimate so that you are 90% confident that your range will include the true value of the quantity.

1. The air distance in statute miles from Moscow to Santiago.
2. The number of gold medals won in the summer Olympic Games by Finnish competitors from 1896 to 1992.
3. The area of Greenland in square miles.
4. The year the ballpoint pen was invented.

5. The year that the H.J. Heinz food manufacturing company was founded.
6. The population of Belize in 1990.
7. Denmark's gross national product (in US dollars) in 1989.
8. The year that Louis Braille, inventor of the Braille communication system, was born.
9. The average depth of the Pacific ocean in feet (to the nearest thousand).
10. The length in miles of the river Danube.

Now, turn to Appendix B to find out the right answers. Next, count the number of times that the true answer fell outside your range for each of the ten questions. If your confidence was appropriate, then no more than one of the ten answers should have been wrong i.e. only one of your ten answers should have fallen outside the range that you gave. If you are like participants in my MBA and executive programmes, then many more than one of your ten answers will have been wrong. In my classroom demonstrations of this, I give the true answer after every question is asked, so giving participants the broad hint to widen their range when subsequent questions are asked. But it makes no difference. Managers don't know when they don't know the answer. They are, generally, overconfident in that they feel that they do, in fact, know the answer and so produce upper and lower bounds that are too narrow and often don't contain the true answer. In other words, they feel confident that they do know the answer but actually don't: they don't know that they don't know.

Overconfidence

How does this overconfidence occur? Several influences have been identified. The first links to behaviour of waiters in restaurants. Consider thought problem 6.

Thought problem 6

Imagine that you are a waiter in a busy restaurant and, because you cannot give good service to all the people who sit at the tables that you serve, you use your judgement to identify those people who will leave good tips or poor tips. You have developed this ability to a great extent, and those people who you predict will tip well mostly do. Conversely, those who you predict won't tip mostly don't. Are your judgemental predictions accurate?

Yes, they are – but note that the waiter will give good service to those he or she thinks will tip well, and ignore those who he or she thinks will not tip. If the quality of service in itself has an effect on whether or not a customer tips, then the waiter's actions will, by themselves, determine the tipping outcome. The only true way that the waiter can test out the quality of his or her judgement is to give poor service to good tip prospects and excellent service to poor tip prospects.[2]

Outside the restaurant business, the decision to hire new employees is an analogous situation. Most of us feel that we are able to interview fairly, and feel comfortable with our hiring decisions: we can identify appropriate employees. But we seldom hear what about happened to the candidates that we declined. It follows that the only true test of our interviewing capabilities is to hire those that we feel we should reject.

Try the following thought problem:[3]

Thought problem 7

Imagine four cards, each with a letter of the alphabet written on one side and a number on the other side. Four cards lie on the table in front of you, and you see the following characters.

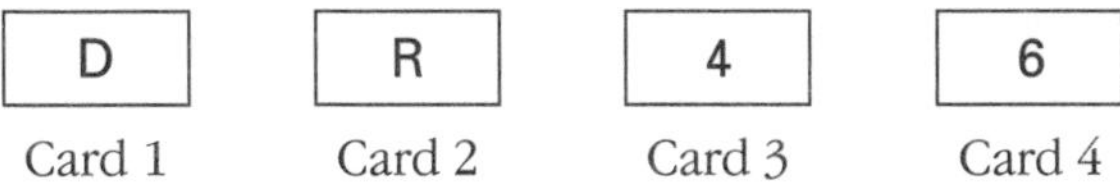

Now think of the rule, if a card has a 'D' on the side then it has a '4' on the other. Which of the four cards needs to be turned over in order to find out whether the rule is true or false? You can choose one card, two cards, three cards, or all four cards – but choose only those cards that are critical to testing whether the rule is true or false.

If you are like most people who have tried this thought problem, then you will say that only the 'D' must be turned, or else the 'D' and the '4'. But turning the 4 is irrelevant to testing the rule, since the rule would allow any letter to be on the back of the card. Most individuals do not choose the card '6', which could well demonstrate that the rule is false. In other words, we tend to test our beliefs in a manner that does not maximise the chances of falsification. We look to confirm our beliefs rather than disconfirm them.

Confirmation bias

In another demonstration of what has been called the 'confirmation bias', I tell my class that I have a rule in mind that classifies sets of three integers, which I call triples.[4] I call out an example of a triple that has been produced by my rule: 2, 4, 6. Members of the class are told to try and discover my rule by generating other triples to give me to test – I will say whether they conform to my rule. I tell members of the class not to call out what they think my rule is until they are certain that they have deduced it. My rule is simply, 'any ascending sequence', but most participants think that the rule is more complex and go on to test triples such as 4, 8, 12, or 20, 40, 60, etc. Eventually, they announce their rule and are convinced of its correctness. In other words, people tend to think of only positive tests of their view of the rule that can never be falsified: a bias toward confirmation, rather than disconfirmation, of our decisions.

This result suggests that without prompting, we are unlikely, as waiters, to give service to those predicted to be poor tippers or, as interviewers, to hire those we view as poor prospects.

So, the conclusion is that we don't place ourselves in situations where we can test the quality of our judgement. We seek out only that information that will confirm the quality of our predictions and decisions – like the way in which we will tend to read adverts only about the car that we have just purchased rather than those that describe the virtues of the cars that we recently chose not to buy.[5]

Hindsight bias

But the picture is bleaker. In one famous study,[6] MBA students were asked to predict in the early 1970s possible outcomes of President Nixon's immediately forthcoming trip to China. Would a named treaty be signed? Would the president visit a named city? Many questions of this sort were posed. The students wrote down their predictions, and were also asked to put a confidence figure next to each prediction. Two weeks then elapsed and the students returned to the MBA classroom. Unexpectedly, the same students were asked to recall their confidence estimates, given that the named events had or had not happened. The events that had occurred were reported widely in the press at that time.

The findings were instructive – if an event had in fact occurred, then the students tended to recollect that they had predicted it with a high degree of confidence when, in fact, they hadn't. If a named event had not occurred, then the students felt that they had not predicted it or, if they recalled that they had, they also recalled placing a low degree of confidence on this poor prediction. However, a check on their actual predictions revealed the contrary – a higher degree of confidence that the named events would occur. In short, the students evidenced what has been termed the 'I-knew-it-all-along effect' – or 'hindsight bias'. So in general, we don't learn from experience because experience has little to teach us: our *recollections* of our judgemental predictions 'confirm' these to have been accurate.

Expert predictions

Are predictions of the future by experts any more accurate? Consider the following newspaper articles in which predictions of UK house prices were made in the period between May 1991 and November 1992. As you will see, these predictions contrast with the reality, which was that house prices in the UK peaked in the second quarter of 1989. From this time until the first quarter of 1993, when prices levelled out and began to rise again, the average loss in price was 36% (source: Nationwide Building Society, Historical House Price Series).

'City: Halifax says house prices rise in April', the *Daily Telegraph*, 4 May 1991 (© 1991 the *Telegraph* plc, London)

House prices in Britain rose 0.2 p.c. in April, but remain 1.1 p.c. lower than this time last year, according to the latest index from the Halifax Building Society. The underlying trend is still weak, with prices on a seasonally adjusted basis falling 0.5 p.c. in the month.

However, the society believes that with the prospect of further interest rate reductions over the next few months, an increase in buying activity should gradually feed through, with prices forecast to rise 5 p.c. by the year-end.

'House prices expected to go up 12 per cent. We expect to see turnover pick up slowly during the summer with prices starting to move up in the early part of next year' by Richard Northedge, the *Daily Telegraph*, 13 May 1991 (© 1991 the *Telegraph* plc, London)

A 12 per cent rise in house prices next year is forecast today by Lloyds Bank. Prices and the levels of sales have been depressed since 1988, but [Lloyds Bank] bank economist, says: 'We expect to see turnover pick up slowly during the summer with prices starting to move up in the early part of the next year.'

'City: House prices set to rise', the *Daily Telegraph*, 3 June 1991 (© 1991 the *Telegraph* plc, London)

A new wave of house inflation may be on the way as interest rates fall, warns a report today from Business Strategies, the economic consultants.

The report says that high interest rates have capped rather than reduced the pressure for homes but a changing demand profile will result in a big increase in the accommodation needed for single people.

'House prices rise two per cent as buyers return' by Ian Cowie, the *Daily Telegraph*, 4 June 1991 (© 1991 the *Telegraph* plc, London)

The house price index compiled by the Nationwide Anglia Building Society rose by two per cent last month, the largest increase for more than a year.

'We may be seeing the beginning of a modest recovery in the market,' said (the) retail director of the society ... 'There are some signs of greater activity as the mortgage interest rate cuts start to work their way through to the housing market.'

'Family finance: home loans key to house prices. Imaginative mortgage schemes are attracting buyers back into the housing market and giving it a gentle fillip, says Jeff Prestridge' by Jeff Prestridge, the *Sunday Telegraph*, 7 July 1991 (© 1991 the *Telegraph* plc, London)

The housing market, savaged over the past three years by sky-high mortgage rates and plummeting property values, is slowly recovering. So say Abbey National, National Westminster Bank and Nationwide Building Society, which all reported last week on the outlook for property and house prices.

Nationwide, which reported a 3.1 per cent year-on-year tumble in house prices, is optimistic the market is on the brink of a revival. 'The recent series of mortgage interest rate cuts is helping to strengthen the housing market,' said (the Society) 'and they should increase levels of activity.'

Cornerstone, the estate agency arm of Abbey, is equally confident. 'We have seen an increase in first-time buyer confidence,' it claimed. 'Quicker sales and greater number of buyers for flats and terraced houses are now beginning to impact on other sectors of the market.'

'House prices falling by 21/22pc says Halifax' by Ian Cowie, the *Daily Telegraph*, 10 October 1991 (© 1991 the *Telegraph* plc, London)

House prices are falling at the rate of 2.5 per cent a year and may end 1991 lower than they started, the Halifax Building Society said yesterday.

The forecast represents a U-turn by Britain's biggest mortgage lender. Last year it said: 'A slight fall in base rates followed by a further 2 per cent to 3 per cent off next year could see house prices rising by over 5 per cent by the end of 1991.

Since then, base rates have been cut by 3.5 percentage points and mortgage rates eased by 3 percentage points. But the Halifax says the average house price has fallen by £1,685 to £65,730.

Nationwide Anglia, the second largest building society, predicted at Christmas that prices would rise by 10 per cent this year. But it is now more pessimistic…

'The Halifax is now expecting house prices to rise by somewhat less than 3 per cent in 1991 with a slight fall during the year a distinct possibility.'

'City: It's backs to the wall for Britain's home owners. With house prices continuing to fall, Robert Tyerman examines the effect of the slump and how much longer mortgage holders may have to suffer before the long hoped for revival begins' by Robert Tyerman, the *Sunday Telegraph*, 8 March 1992 (© 1992 the *Telegraph* plc, London)

News last week from one of the top building societies that house prices are continuing to slip brought many up with a jolt … Wriglesworth sees a further 2 per cent house price fall this year – or between 6 and 7 per cent in real terms. 'There is no prospect of a recovery for two years,' he declares. And he warns that if the downward spiral intensifies and prices tumble by as much as 10, 15 or even 20 per cent, the banks and building societies whose loans helped fuel the 1980s property boom could face 'meltdown'.

'Family Finance: How to cash in on the Tory win. House prices, equities, savings – all should benefit from the election result. Jeff Prestridge polls the experts to find ways in which investors can benefit too' by Jeff Prestridge, the *Sunday Telegraph* London, 12 April 1992 (© 1992 the *Telegraph* plc, London)

... Halifax and Nationwide both reported further falls in prices last week – Halifax a 5 per cent fall in the year to March and Nationwide a 2.7 per cent drop in the first quarter.

Experts now feel prices should move upwards by the end of the year. 'The end of uncertainty will help increase confidence in the housing market', says Halifax. ... 'Housing activity will increase, which should mean house prices will be trending upwards by the end of the year. We are predicting house price increases of between 3 per cent and 4 per cent year-on-year by the turn of the year.'

... of mortgage broker John Charcol says: 'The election outcome should establish a bottom to the housing market. Having seen significant house price falls in the first three months of this year, we now think there will be a compensating increase in the last six months of the year.'

Like Halifax, he is forecasting a 3 per cent to 4 per cent uplift.

'Average house prices fall by record 3pc in a month' by Ian Cowie, the *Daily Telegraph*, 10 October 1992 (© 1992 the *Telegraph* plc, London)

... But housing analyst ... at UBS Phillips & Drew said: 'This is extremely bad news, especially as September is usually a seasonally good month in the year. The underlying trend in house prices is strongly downward.

'We expect a mild bounce back in October, partly as a consequence of the recent mortgage rate cut, but predict the annual fall in house prices will still be at least seven per cent at the end of this year.

'We do not believe there will be any significant house price recovery before 1994 unless the Government produces a major fiscal kick start to the housing market – which is unlikely, given its Public Sector Borrowing Requirement constraints. We expect a further five per cent fall in prices during 1993.'

... said: 'It is not unreasonably pessimistic to predict a seven per cent fall this year with five per cent more to come off next year.'

'Record fall for house prices' by Teresa Hunter, the *Guardian*, 10 October 1992 (Copyright 1992 the *Guardian*)

One Phillips & Drew building society analyst said he expected prices to fall 5 per cent next year, after finishing 1992 7 per cent lower than they began it …

'Council tax will mean new fall in house prices' by Andrew Grice and David Smith, *The Times*, 22 November 1992 (Copyright 1992 Times Newspapers Ltd.)

… Morgan Grenfell, the merchant bank, says the value of houses in London and the southeast will fall by up to 4.5% next year as the switch to a tax on property deters people from 'trading up' in the already depressed housing market. House prices will drop by up to 4% in the southwest, 3.5% in East Anglia, the Midlands and northwest, and 3% in the north …

'House prices "will continue to slide". Report says 20pc of home-owners will be in debt trap' by Teresa Hunter and Frank Kane, the *Guardian*, 30 November 1992 (Copyright 1992 the *Guardian*)

House prices will continue to fall next year by at least 5 per cent, particularly in the South, leaving one in five homeowners caught in a debt trap, according to a report by ..., an analyst at UBS Phillips & Drew.

Prices will begin to rise in 1994, but they will end that year roughly where they are now. The mid-1990s could see a mini property boom, although not on the scale of that of the last decade …

The worst price falls will be in the already hard-hit south of England. Prices in Greater London will end 1993 at 7 per cent lower than they began it, while prices in the South-east, South-west and East Anglia will be 6 per cent down at the end of the year.

In the North, property prices will fall by 5 per cent, and by 6 per cent in the North-west, while the smallest falls will be in Scotland and Northern Ireland where prices will decline by 1 per cent and 3 per cent respectively …

Now try thought problem 8.

Thought problem 8

How do you rate yourself as a car driver? (tick a box)

Well below average	☐	☐	☐	☐	☐	☐	☐	☐	☐	☐	☐	☐	Well above average

Average

If you are like most of the people who have answered this question, then you will have ticked a box to the right-hand side of average. But, by definition, we can't all be above average! In another study, budding entrepreneurs were interviewed about their chances of business success.[7] But their estimates were unrelated to objective predictors, such as post-school education, prior supervisory experience, or initial capital. Moreover, more than 80% of them described their chances of success as 70% or better, whilst the true five-year survival rate for new businesses is, in fact, as low as 33%.

Alleviating overconfidence

We have a strong tendency to see an individual forecasting problem as a unique one-off event rather than as instances of a broader class of events. We tend to pay particular attention to the special features of the single event we are called upon to forecast rather than attempting to consider either (i) our past success at predicting similar events, or (ii) base-rate occurrences for such similar events. To see this, consider a gambler betting on the spin of a roulette wheel. If the roulette wheel has produced an outcome of red for the last ten spins, then the gambler may feel that his or her confidence for black on the next spin should be higher than that for red. However, ask the same gambler the relative proportions of red to black on spins of the wheel and they will probably answer '50–50'.

Since the roulette ball has no memory, it follows that the latter relative frequency assessment is a more accurate one.[8]

Consider the next thought problem:

> ***Thought problem 9***
>
> Linda is 31 years old, single, outspoken and very bright. She has a degree in philosophy. As a student, she was deeply concerned with issues of discrimination and social justice, and also participated in anti-nuclear demonstrations. Which is most likely:
>
> (a) Linda is a bank teller.
> (b) Linda is a bank teller who is active in the feminist movement?

When this problem was given to MBA students,[9] almost 90% of those asked thought that it was more probable that Linda was a bank teller who was active in the feminist movement. But this answer is wrong. The co-occurrence of 'bank teller' and 'feminist' cannot be more probable than each event on its own. For example, the probability that your line manager is female and married must be less than the probability that your line manager is female. It seems that respondents thought about problem 9 by judging how close each of the options (a) and (b) was to the earlier description of Linda. However, if the question 'Which of the alternatives is more probable?' is replaced by the words 'There are 100 people who fit the description above. How many of them are (a) bank tellers, (b) bank tellers and active in the feminist movement?', then the percentage of individuals who violate the probability logic drops to less than 25%. Clearly, instructions to assess a frequency (i.e. how many?) facilitates more accurate thinking than instructions to assess a subjective probability[8] (i.e. which of the alternatives is more probable?).

Overall, managers don't seem to be able to make good estimates of the likelihood of unique events. When faced with the need to make such forecasts, we tend to pay particular attention to the distinguishing features of the problem in hand and reject analogies to other instances of the same type as superficial. But research shows that we should draw such analogies.

In summary, we advocate that in assessing your confidence in a forecast or prediction, you attempt to locate a reference class of previous forecasts that you have made that are similar to the event that you now need to predict. If you have received timely feedback on the accuracy of your earlier forecasts, then the prediction task is likely to be like that of professional weather forecasting – where accurate forecasting is a general finding. If not, then you should consider whether there is an historic relative frequency reference class that you can use. For example, if you are considering the likelihood that a newly hired worker will stay for at least a year, then you should consider the number of workers who have been hired in your organisation at that grade (i.e. identify the reference class) and then calculate how many in, say, the last five years have remained for at least one year.

If a reference class of previous forecasts or historic frequencies is not obvious, then be aware that the only way to assess the likelihood of the event is to use judgement – but judgement can lead to bias, as we have shown in this chapter.

However, many strategic decisions that involve consideration of the evolving business environment do not lend themselves to prediction by relative frequencies. Often, best-guess predictions of unique, one-off events are made using judgement. Turn back to Chapter 2, where we quoted from the *Newsweek* analysis of the events leading up to Saddam Hussein's invasion of Kuwait.

Clearly, overconfidence is evident. How, then, should the leaders of organisations forecast the future? If judgement is so poor, and best-guess forecasts for unique events can be so far off target, should the future be predicted instead by the throw of a die or the toss of a coin? In other words, are we so ill-equipped to forecast the future that we shouldn't bother? Fortunately, one technique has been shown to aid managers make strategic decisions in the face of uncertainty about the future without requiring judgements of likelihood or confidence. That technique, scenario planning, is detailed in the next chapter.

For Joe Blott, discussed at the beginning of this chapter, the recommendation is clear. He should be wary that his confidence estimates may, in fact, be overconfident. His recollection of the previous quality of his judgemental predictions may be a product of hindsight bias. He should seek disconfirming evidence that his past predictions were accurate.

Key messages

What lessons can be drawn from this chapter? First, managers are overconfident. Of course, confidence itself is a desirable trait in a leader. The words 'I'm not sure' are more characteristic of followers than decisive leaders. But, as we have seen, confidence in judgement may be unwarranted – we seldom put ourselves in situations that provide a true test of the quality of our predictions and decisions. Additionally, we don't learn from experience – our recollections of our judgemental predictions tend to confirm these as having been accurate. Recall the predictions of residential house price movements as recounted in the newspaper articles. No-one concerned with these predictions – forecasters, newspaper editors or readers – seems to be aware of the wild inaccuracy of the house price forecasts. Have we any reason to believe that the forecasts made in 2001 will be any more accurate? Judgemental predictions for unique, one-off events are likely to be even further off target because there is no relative frequency reference class or historic tally of predictions and subsequent outcomes with which to provide feedback for improving judgemental forecasts.

If you can, locate a reference class of historic frequencies – or outcomes of previous forecasts – that are linked closely to the event that you are trying to predict, and use this reference class instead of your judgement.

FOUR

How to Think with Scenarios

Fred McNulty was CEO of Autotell, a firm that provided the information systems that link together the electromechanical devices that provide cash and account balances to individual customers and are located on the walls outside banks and building societies (automated teller machines, ATMs). These machines function both in and out of office hours. Autotell had a virtual monopoly on providing a service that linked each individual machine with almost all the major banks and building societies in Europe. The future looked rosy to Fred. Every few months, another one of the smaller banks or building societies would become a member of the grouping that controlled Autotell so that its customers could have access to cash at any of the thousands of machines that were linked together by Autotell. Soon, Fred would have total control of all the links in Europe! But where next? Fred knew that Autotell's core competence was in designing and maintaining information systems to link machines with the banks. Most recently, he had tried to diversify by developing a lease-hire of the machines themselves, including the information systems links. But the take-up had been poor. Customers preferred to deal directly with the manufacturers of the machines because of their perceived excellence in servicing the machines when they failed to operate. Fred realised that the machines linked by Autotell provided only a limited service to a bank's customers if they used another bank's machine. In such circumstances, a customer could only withdraw cash and check their account's balance. Other services that customers wanted – like deposits, mini-statements, cheque book ordering and bill payment – were beyond the capabilities of the linking system. Fred was also worried about the potential uptake of electronic purses – cards that could be recharged with a desired amount of money via an Internet or telephone link. Fred knew that in the long term his business depended on the public's continuing desire for ready access to cash. They key issue was clear – what factors would speed up, slow down or sustain this desire? Although the issue was clear, its resolution was much less so. What could help him predict the future?

One approach to help in answering Fred's concerns is to build scenarios. The approach is to build several scenarios of how the future could turn out to be. Each scenario is a pen-picture of a particular future. Several scenarios are constructed since a key aspect of scenario planning is to challenge a single, best guess of what the future will be like. Scenario planning focuses on key certainties and uncertainties about the future, and uses this information to construct pen-pictures in an information-rich way in order to provide vivid descriptions of plausible future worlds.

Scenario planning

In scenario planning, a major focus is on how the future can evolve – from today's point in time to the future that has unfolded in the horizon year, or end state, of the scenario, say ten years later. Essentially, scenario thinking is focused on the reasoning underpinning our judgements about the future. These judgements are separated into those about key uncertainties and those about key certainties – or key trends that are already in the pipeline. These factors are key in that they are seen, by the decision maker, to have a major impact on the issue of concern – in Fred McNulty and Autotell's case, the future of cash. Here, key uncertainties might be the speed of development of the capability of electronic purses; the degree/speed to/by which the public accept these alternatives to cash; and the possibility of a series of high-publicity robberies of individuals while retrieving cash from ATMs.

Key certainties might be the continued use of cash as an untraceable way of paying bills without VAT, and the continued use of cash by those with poor credit ratings. Key trends might be the decreasing costs to the end user of all technological products; the convergence of debit and credit cards to single formats; and the increasing amount of technology being placed on a card – a change from magnetic strips to complex, information-capable chips. The relationship between these three variables – uncertainties, certainties and trends – together with the behaviour of key players in the scenarios who will act to preserve and enhance their own interest within a particular future as it unfolds, are thought through in the process of scenario planning. In the case of Autotell, key players whose actions would need to be considered are: the credit card companies, and the banks who have trialled electronic purses.

Next, we provide a concrete example of a quick way to construct extreme scenarios. Later, we introduce a more sophisticated method of scenario construction, which produces less extreme and arguably more plausible scenarios.

Scenario construction: the extreme-world method

Box 1 lists the eight major steps in the construction of scenarios. The first step is to identify an issue of concern, around which the scenarios will be constructed. Key issues often concern the survival and viability of an organisation, or one of its divisions, in an environment that is known to be changing and which might change in a way as to be inhospitable to that organisation with its current competencies and core capabilities.

In the example we will develop now, the key issue of concern is the survival and profitability of a Europe-based semiconductor manufacturing company.[1] The predetermined elements and trends, as seen by the company's key personnel, are listed in Table 1. The impacts of these trends on the survival and profitability of the particular semiconductor manufacturing company are also given.

Table 2 gives the key uncertainties, the ways in which these uncertainties can resolve themselves, and their impact on the issue of concern.

Box 1 Steps in scenario construction: the extreme-world method

1. Identify the issue of concern and the horizon year that will be captured in the scenarios.
2. Idenify predetermined trends that have some degree of impact on the issue of concern.
3. Identify critical uncertainties, which, when resolved (one way or the other), have some degree of impact on the issue of concern.
4. Identify the degree to which the trends and resolved uncertainties have a negative or positive impact on the issue of concern.
5. Create extreme worlds by putting all positively resolved uncertainties in one scenario and all negatively resolved uncertainties in another scenario.
6. Add the predetermined trends to both scenarios.
7. Check for internal coherence. Could the trends and resolved uncertainties coexist in a plausible future scenario?
8. Add in the actions of individuals and/or organisations who will be impacted by the future described in a scenario. What actions would they take/have taken to satisfy their own interests?

Table 1 *Predetermined trends*

		Impact
T1	Increased product complexity	+
T2	Shortening product lifecycles	+
T3	Increasing demand for cheaper packaging	–
T4	Customers prefer to buy from European suppliers	+
T5	Increasing demand for shorter supply lead time	+
T6	Increasing overall demand for integrated circuits	+
T7	Far East production costs remain lower	–
T8	Low level of local competition	+

Next, the positive impact uncertainties and all the predetermineds are clustered together, and a story line is developed that interlinks as many of these elements as possible. The focus is on developing a plausible chain of events that are, to some degree, causally related

Table 2 *Key uncertainties*

				Impact
U1	EC import duty requirements	u11	Higher	++
		u12	As is	+
		u13	Lower	–
U2	Demand for ceramic device types (replaced by plastics)	u21	Higher	++
		u22	As is	+
		u23	Lower	–
		u24	Very low	– –
U3	Success of new technology	u31	Fast	+
		u32	Slow	–
U4	Reaction of local competition	u41	Strong	–
		u42	Weak	+
U5	Internal corporate volumes	u51	High	+
		u52	Low	–
U6	Internal manufacturing policy	u61	Make	+
		U62	Buy	–

and that show how the future will unfold to result in the *end state* captured within the horizon year of the particular scenario. The same process is then repeated for a negative scenario.

Box 2 gives two illustrative short scenarios based on the trends and uncertainties listed in Tables 1 and 2. The third scenario detailed in Box 2 is an extrapolation of the present and is often called the status quo scenario.

Notice that uncertainty u11 and uncertainty u42 in Table 2 are, to some degree, internally incoherent, i.e. incompatible with each other. For example, if EC import duties were high, then reaction of local competition (i.e. from within the EC) will not be weak. Therefore, this particular combination of resolved uncertainties is not described in the scenarios since it is implausible.

The example scenarios in Box 2 are not developed fully since the reaction of the Far East producers of plastic packaging to the technology boom scenario has not been thought through and incorporated. If the scenarios were developed more fully – we will detail a fully developed one later in this chapter – then the next stage after

Box 2 Three scenarios

Positive Scenario: Technology Boom

New packaging technologies are developed rapidly, and are widely adopted at the expense of the traditional packing methods of plastic and ceramics. Ceramic packaging all but disappears. The overall market demand increases significantly on the back of the improved capabilities of the new technology.

The manufacturing expertise for the new technology resides with only a few key companies worldwide. The new market entry costs are high. EC import duties are maintained at high levels to protect local manufacturing of the new technologies. Vendor choice is dependent on technology advantage rather than price.

The corporation is able to exploit this trend by leveraging its established skill base. All new products are manufactured internally with the scope to convert existing products and bring their manufacture back in house.

Negative Scenario: Plastics Dominate

Plastic packaging technology has resolved power dissipation and high pincount difficulties. Virtually all packaging applications are now in plastic. The overall market volume expands rapidly. Ceramic packaging all but disappears. New technologies such as multichip modules (MCMs) and chip on board (COB) are slow to realise their potential.

The manufacturing expertise and infrastructure to manufacture the new plastic packages reside only in the Far East. EC regulations abolish import duties on packaged semiconductor devices. Customers would prefer to buy in Europe but can't; virtually all subcontract assembly is carried out in the Far East.

Faced with an erosion of the competitive advantage of its ceramic manufacturing expertise, the corporation has no choice but to switch to plastic packaging for all products. All package manufacturing is subcontracted out to Far East operators. The internal skill base and manufacturing infrastructure disappears.

Status Quo Scenario: Business as Usual

The overall demand for semiconductor devices continues to increase at the current rate. The demand for ceramic packages remains at the current levels with moderate increases in the higher pincount package styles. The remainder of the market is dominated by plastic packages, especially small outline products. Opportunities for new packaging technologies such as MCM and COB remain limited.

There is no significant change in EC import duty regulations, and therefore little change in the cost differential between manufacturing in Europe and the Far East. European subcontractors are used for prototyping and low-volume work, while the larger production volumes are sent to the Far East. Entry barriers for new competitors remain high. The corporation continues to manufacture its complex, leading-edge products internally. The remainder are assembled either internally or externally, depending on cost. Overall volumes are maintained at current levels.

the construction of the scenarios is complete is to utilise them in a decision-making process.

Using scenarios in decision making

There are two ways in which scenarios can be used in decision making. The first is to test the viability of a current business idea against the plausible futures represented in the scenarios. In the abstract analytical sense, a business can be thought of as a business idea. A business idea is the systemic linking of the business's competencies and strengths. For example, a business idea for a business school could be that illustrated in Figure 1.

Here, the strengths that the business school possesses are summarised in short statements. The impact of the deployment of these strengths produces revenue, and the reinvestment of the revenue produced produces a self-reinforcing cycle or positive feedback loop that would, in a stable environment, be a robust business idea that would become less and less replicable by competitors – without serious investment from a competitor school – over a period of time.

Overall, a business idea should specify three major elements of a business's attempt to be successful:

- The *competitive advantage* that is aimed for – in the case of the business school, this is a product that is differentiated from its competitors.
- The *distinctive competencies* on which the first point is based – for example, an ability to attract top national academics.
- The *growth* mechanism – a positive feedback loop.

If the business school was part of a wider university, then utilisation of the school's revenue to support finiancially weaker academic areas would, of course, weaken the positive feedback loop for the school itself.

However, notice that if the external environment were to change –

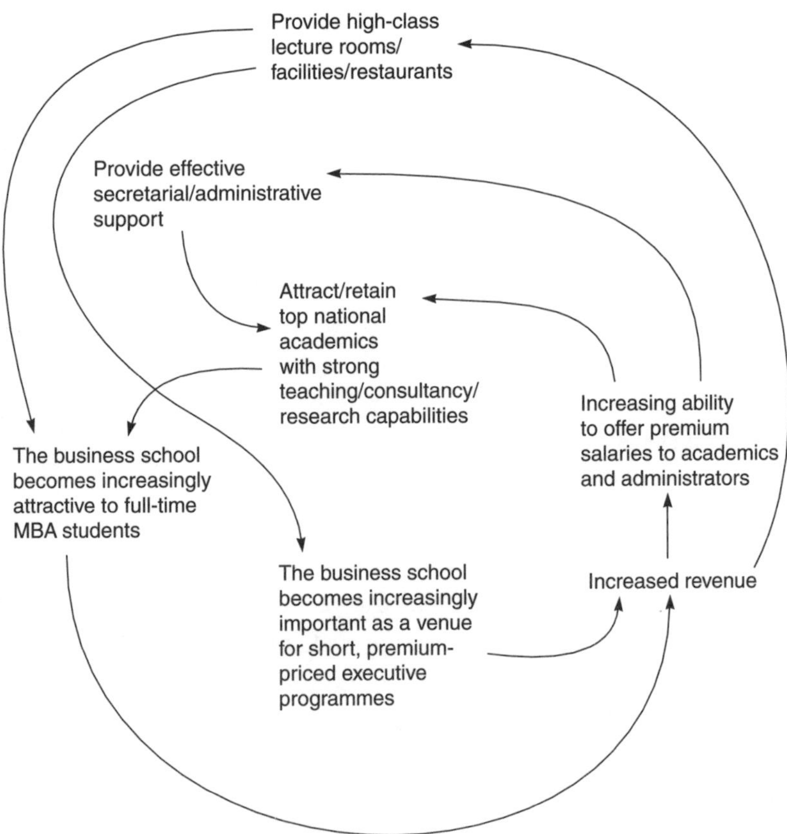

Figure 1 *An illustrative business idea for a business school.*

say, technological developments enabled students to engage in video conferencing with internationally recognised academics across the world, and these new technologies were easy to deploy in the students' own homes – then perhaps the current business idea – with its emphasis on employing full-time academics and providing attractive learning environments for students who are able to physically attend the business school – would appear less robust. Creating such plausible futures and testing the essence of the business – the business idea – against them is one use of scenario planning in a decision process.

Kees van der Heijden[2] has likened the testing of business ideas against scenarios to 'windtunnelling'. Here, the business idea is analogous to the design of an aeroplane. The scenarios are analogous to wind conditions – some are more extreme than others but all are plausible conditions under which the airplane must be able to fly. Under some wind conditions, the plane may be harder to keep airborne, but essentially its airframe (i.e. business idea) must be robust.

The second way to utilise the scenarios in a decision process is to evaluate lower-level strategies or decisions. In the business school example, this might be an evaluation of a decision option to focus research and development (R&D) investment on producing CD-ROM versions of course materials. In the semiconductor manufacturing company example, it might be the decision option of maintaining or increasing investment in new ceramic packaging production technology. Essentially, a current strategy, a contemplated strategy, or a range of alternative strategies can be evaluated for robustness against constructed scenarios. Table 3 gives a matrix representation of this evaluation process.

Often, no one strategy performs well against the whole range of constructed scenarios. If you consider strategies 1, 2 and 3, you can see that strategy 1 maximises the minimum pay-off. Given a simple choice between strategies 1, 2 and 3, strategy 1 would seem the most robust choice if we felt it was not possible to say that one scenario was more likely than another – recall that this is an explicit assumption underpinning scenario planning as a technique for dealing with uncertainty.

Table 3 *Testing the robustness of strategies against scenarios*

	Scenario 1	Scenario 2	Scenario 3
Strategy 1	✓✓✓	✓	✗
Strategy 2	✗✗	✓	✓
Strategy 3	✓✓	✗✗	✓✓✓
New strategy	✓✓✓	✓✓✓	✓✓✓

Note, however, that there is an additional row in Table 3, entitled 'new strategy', which the very act of scenario planning may incubate in the mind of the decision maker as he or she ponders the set of plausible futures encapsulated in the scenarios. This ability of scenario planning to stimulate creative thinking is perhaps best illustrated by a 'real' scenario (Box 3). This scenario was one of several constructed for a corporation that was involved in moving raw materials and finished goods around the globe.[3] The company was concerned with the (re)location of its major depots so that they would be at the hubs of future trading networks. It follows that the scenarios were constructed to represent plausible future trading patterns in the EC and the rest of the world. The corporation tested the robustness of choice of alternative countries and cities against the scenarios. Several cities that were not in the choice set before the scenario construction became favourites in the subsequent decision process since they were found to be robust against a range of plausible future world trading patterns. These trading patterns were encapsulated and bounded by the scenarios that were constructed to capture the range of plausible futures.

So far, we have described one method to bound these futures – a simplified method that uses an extreme positive scenario, an extreme negative scenario, and a more neutral status quo or business-as-usual scenario. Some practitioners of scenario planning caution against presenting the decision maker with such extreme worlds since their very extremeness may cause doubts among their clients – the business managers – about their plausibility. Another way to construct scenarios that has found favour among practitioners is described next.

Box 3 A 'real' scenario of future trading patterns

Global Perspective

World economic growth picked up appreciably from 2002 onwards – driven by the success in bilateral trade talks, a surge in US exports, a strengthening employment situation in Europe, and lowering real costs of oil.

The signs of economic recovery were reflected in a rapid growth in global trade. The trade among developed economies continues to dominate, but an increasing proportion of the expanding markets involve developing countries. Institutions, frustrated by low interest rates in the developed countries and encouraged by opportunities in the less developed countries, invest many billions of dollars of their managed funds in the newly created financial institutions and ventures around the world. Latin America and central Europe (increasingly integrated with the European Community) are the major beneficiaries.

Japan's new-found market liberalism and détente with the USA reinforce general optimism about the future. Japan's proximity to the potentially massive consumer markets in Russia and China led the Japanese government to sanction heavy investment in these countries and to build up the commercial infrastructure around Maizuru, facing the expanding container port of Vostochny on Russia's east coast.

Western Europe's high direct production costs continue to reduce its competitiveness in the world. Lower direct costs in central and eastern Europe offer a competitive lifeline for western European manufacturers, a lifeline they take with some alacrity. Foreign direct investment increases significantly in terms of increased joint ventures and wholly owned subsidiaries. Pressure is applied successfully to speed up the process of integration of Poland, Hungary and the Czech Republic. Western exports to Russia of consumer goods also increase rapidly. Belarussia and the Baltic states benefit from their geographic siting in attracting infrastructure investment and aid from the West.

Hungary continues to attract the majority of investment from the USA, but its partners in the Vise-Grad Triangle rapidly close the gap opened up in the first half of the decade.

The EC and US axis (which successfully argued concessions in addition to GATT from their G7 partners) resolve to further reduce market access barriers. G7 initiated gilt-edged guarantees to the developing countries, and attractive non-reciprocal trade arrangements persuaded many of the less-developed countries to reduce their own trade barriers. This has mutual benefits, but more importantly promotes an atmosphere of trust and the first real moves toward comprehensive credit union agreement.

Regional Perspective

Since the necessary constitutional and legislative reforms have been carried out in the first half of the decade, the more advanced developing countries in central and eastern Europe achieve acceptable political stability and continue to maintain tight fiscal policies under guidelines set by the International Monetary Fund (IMF). The situation continues to improve in the second half of the decade. There is a general commitment by the governments of the countries to liberalisation policies, and the move to democracy continues, thus speeding up the accomplishment of the privatisation process. This results in expansion of the private sector into the majority of services and industries before the turn of the century.

Although aid provided by the industrialised countries remains weak due to their own internal problems during the recession, EC aid increased from the second half of the decade. Germany, in particular, provides aid for Hungary and the Czech Republic.

Institutional investment and foreign direct investment also pick up considerably in the second half of the decade as the emerging financial system and markets of Vise-Grad Triangle countries, Belarussia and Russia, became more attractive to the investors as compared with the traditional markets in developed countries. The EC brings forward negotiations for a free trade agreement with the Vise-Grad Triangle and Russia since it was willing to open up its market to exports from these countries. This increases their ability to pay for their imports and restructuring.

In central Europe, consumer confidence grows rapidly as clear indications are seen of increased prosperity in the region. In the East, Russia recovers its economic balance and growth in GDP, and again begins to grow in importance to the countries in eastern Europe, particularly in terms of consumer markets.

Scenario construction: the driving-forces method

This method has much in common with the first method, in that the critical elements in the decomposition process are predetermineds and uncertainties. However, in the driving forces method, degrees of predictability and uncertainty are allowable, and the outputs of the scenario construction process are not, usually, extreme scenarios. Nevertheless, the output scenarios from this method also bound the perceived uncertainties in a similar way to the scenarios produced in the extreme-world scenario construction method that we discussed earlier.

Figure 2 gives an example structure of four scenarios for the (then) future of South Africa, which are driven by the forces whether or not there is a negotiated settlement, whether or not the transition to majority rule is rapid, and whether or not the economic policies of the majority government are short- or long-term.[4]

Box 4 details the scenarios that were constructed by a team led by Adam Kahane in mid-1991. The horizon year of the scenarios is 2002. These scenarios of the social and political environment in South Africa would be useful to an international company considering three decision options: whether to maintain, reduce or increase its investments and overall presence in South Africa.

Box 5 gives the key steps in the driving forces method.

Within the 12 steps listed in Box 5, note that step 1 is analogous to step 1 in the extreme-world methodology, which we described earlier in Box 1. At step 2 in the driving-forces scenario structuring method, a multitude of elements will emerge from a group brainstorm about the issue of concern. Many of the elements that emerge will address the external environment, in that the predetermineds and uncertainties are not under the control of the individual, group or organisation that they will affect. These are the elements that it may be appropriate to incorporate in the scenarios and these elements should be carried forward to step 3. Other elements will be concerned with areas where the individual/group/organisation has control, i.e. they are decision or strategy options. Since decisions and strategies are to

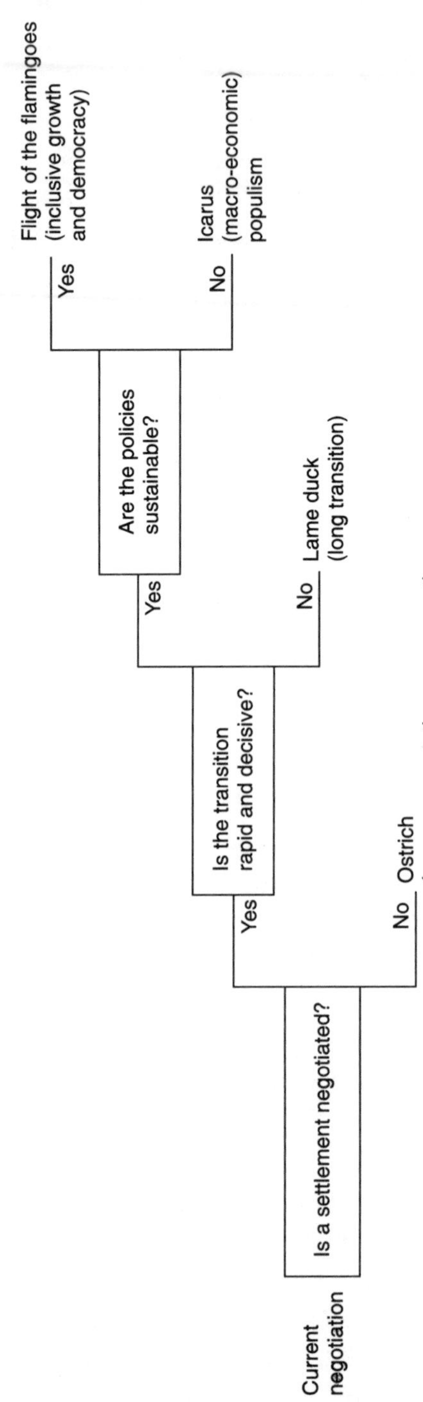

Figure 2 *An output of a driving-forces scenario structuring methodology.*

Box 4 Adam Kahane's four South African scenarios

Scenario 1: Ostrich

As a result of the steps taken by the de Klerk government and the outcome of the white referendum, the international community becomes more tolerant towards white South Africa, and the National Party in particular.

In light of this, the government hardens its negotiation position. At the same time, the liberation movement is perceived to be too radical and loses support internationally. The liberation movements maintained their bottom line. A stand-off results and constitutional negotiations break down.

The government decides to form a new moderate alliance government, which is unacceptable to the liberation movements. This results in mass resistance, which the state suppresses by force.

Although large-scale sanctions are not reimposed, the economy remains in the doldrums because of massive resistance to the new constitution. This resistance leads to escalating repression and violence, and the business climate worsens. This in turn leads to economic stagnation and decline, accompanied by a flight of capital and skills.

The government also fails to deliver on the social front. Resistance and unrest rendered effective social spending impossible, and large outlays are required merely to maintain the status quo. Because society's major inequalities are not addressed, the vicious cycle continues. Eventually, the various parties are forced back to the negotiation table, but under worse social, political and economic conditions than before.

Scenario 2: Lame Duck

Various forces and considerations drive the major parties towards a negotiated settlement. The present government, for example, recognises the necessity or inevitability of extending full political rights to the disenfranchised, but fear is shared by some of the major international actors.

On the other hand, the liberation movement fears the return to repressive minority rule if they do not make significant compromises. Such considerations lead to a transitional arrangement with a variety of sunset clauses, slowly phasing out elements of the present system, as well as minority vetoes and other checks and balances aimed at preventing irresponsible government.

Such a long transition of enforced coalition incapacitates the government because of lowest-common-denominator decision making, which results in indecisive policies. It purports to respond to all, but satisfies none. In consequence, the social and economic crises are addressed inadequately.

Although the transitional government succeeds in being goal directed and effective, it is incapacitated because of the logic of a long transition. Uncertainty grows on the nature of the government that will emerge after the transition.

Regardless of how moderate the declarations of the majority parties in the coalition may be, fears of radical economic policies after the period of a long transition remain. Investors hold back, and there is insufficient growth and development.

Scenario 3: Icarus

In this scenario, a popularly elected democratic government tries to achieve too much too quickly. It had noble origins and good intentions, but it pays insufficient attention to economic forces.

The government embarks on a massive spending spree to meet all the backlogs inherited from the past. It implements food subsidies and price and exchange controls, and institutes other 'quick fix' policies.

The initial results are spectacular growth, increased living standards, improved social conditions, little or no increase in inflation, and increased political support.

But after a year or two, the programme runs into budgetary, monetary and balance of payments constraints. The budget deficit well exceeded 10%. Depreciations, inflation, economic uncertainty and collapse follow. The country experiences an economic crisis of hitherto unknown proportions, which results in social collapse and political chaos.

At this point, the government either does a 180 degree about-turn (while appealing to the International Monetary Fund and the World Bank for assistance), or it is removed from office. The result is a return to authoritarianism and an abandonment of the noble intentions that originally prevailed.

Scenario 4: Flight of the Flamingoes

Flamingoes characteristically take off slowly, fly high and fly together.

A decisive political settlement followed by good government creates conditions in which an initially slow but sustainable economic and social take-off become possible. The key to the government's success is its ability to combine strategies that lead to significant improvements in social delivery with policies that create confidence in the economy.

Access to world markets and relative regional stability are gained, but South Africa does not receive massive overseas investments or aid on the scale of a Marshall Plan.

The government adopts sound social and economic policies and observes macro-economic constraints. It succeeds in curbing corruption in government and raises efficiency levels.

It makes well-targeted social investments, which lead to a decrease in violence and give people confidence that many of the social needs will be met in the longer term.

Once business is convinced that policies will remain consistent in the years ahead, investment grows and employment increases. Initially, this growth is slow, because confidence does not return overnight, but over the years higher rates of growth are attained, and an average rate of growth of close to 5% is realised over the period.

The overall income of the upper income groups grows between 1 and 3% a year.

be evaluated against the scenarios at the final step, these decision options should be removed at step 2 and reconsidered in the final step of the scenario planning process, when such options are evaluated for robustness against the range of constructed futures.

In the scenario planning workshops that we provide at the Graduate School of Business, we also, as standard practice, invite remarkable people to provide insights to our process of scenario building. For example, if one of the driving forces identified at step 6 concerned the speed of the public's take-up of a newly developed technology – say video phones – then we would ask someone with expertise in this technology's development to a question-and-answer

Box 5 Steps in scenario construction using the driving-force method

1. Identify the issue of concern and the horizon year that will be captured in the scenarios.
2. List anything that seems related to the issue of concern. Write each element on a post-it note.
3. Place each post-it note on the scenario structuring space below in relation to its perceived predictability/unpredictability and low impact/high impact on the issue of concern.

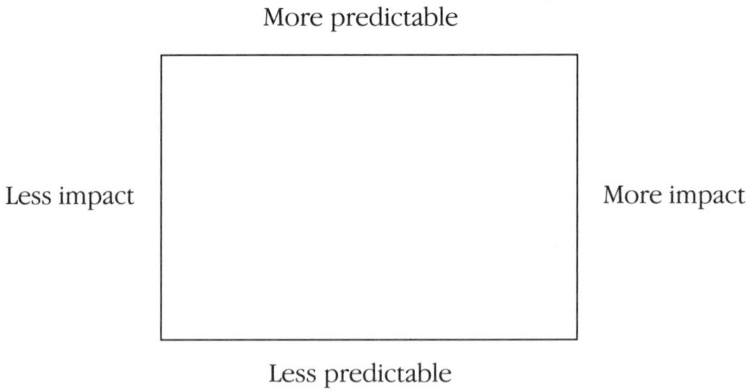

More predictable

Less impact | More impact

Less predictable

4. Focus on the post-its in the bottom right-hand corner, i.e. high-impact/low-predictability events. Try and cluster these post-its into groups of interrelated events, such that the notes in one grouping are interrelated among themselves but unrelated to those in other groupings.
5. From these clusters, try and identify a smaller number of underlying driving forces that link these uncertainties/events at a deeper level.
6. Of the driving forces identified, which two or three really would make a difference to the decision maker and their business?
7. For each driving force, try to capture the range of outcomes by two extremes.
8. Experiment by thinking of combinations of the extremes of one of the driving forces with the extremes of each of the other driving forces. From these experiments, develop the skeletons of three or four scenarios. Select short, catchy names that encapsulate the essence of the scenarios.

9. Inspect post-it notes in the three other quadrants of the scenario structuring space. Place these elements into one or more of the skeleton scenarios created in step 8, in order to flesh them out. Check that elements contained in the top left quadrant could, in principle, appear in any of the skeleton scenarios. If not, reconsider the coherence of the elements of each scenario.
10. Begin to develop each scenario 'storyline'. One way to start this process is to place all the elements within a scenario along a timeline that starts at today's point in time and ends at the point in time captured in the scenario horizon year. Look for causality between elements. Storylines are more plausible when (some) elements are causally related. Time precedence is often a good cue to potential causality.
11. Review the scenarios in light of their utilisation of the original elements in the bottom right-hand quadrant of the scenario structuring space. Are all the high impact / low predictability elements bounded by the range of scenarios that have been constructed? If not, consider creating more scenarios to capture and structure the remaining elements in the quadrant.
12. Evaluate the business idea or strategic options against the futures represented in the scenarios.

session held in conjunction with the executives who comprise the scenario team. After such expert input, the subsequently developed second-generation scenarios will be detailed more fully, and often the ways in which the critical uncertainties may resolve themselves become much clearer.

In our first method for constructing scenarios (see Box 1) we described in step 8 a method of including those individuals/organisations who would be affected by the futures described in the scenarios and would, therefore, act in their own interests as particular futures started to unfold. Another way of capturing degrees of such stakeholder involvement and intervention is to construct a matrix such as that shown in Figure 3.

One of the outputs of step 2 of the driving-forces method will be the names of stakeholders. Those elements can be placed on the stakeholder structuring space[5] of Figure 3 and consulted again after step 9.

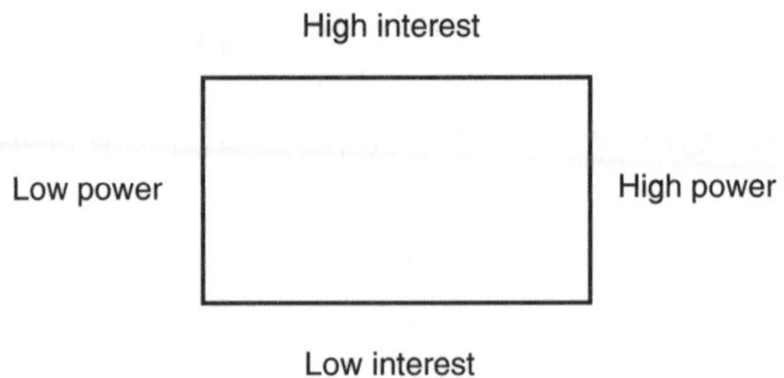

Figure 3 *Stakeholder structuring space.*

As we saw in Figure 2, the outcome of the decision process in scenario planning is the selection of the most robust decision in the face of an unpredictable future. This is also the focus of step 12 in the driving-forces method of scenario construction. An additional focus is on the generation of more robust decision options.

The benefits of scenario planning

However, even if a fundamentally robust option cannot be developed, scenario thinking also provides other benefits. World views can be communicated easily in an organisation via the medium of the scenario stories. Additionally, once a story has been read, and the reasoning underlying its unfolding has been understood, a future has been rehearsed. Thus, once the early events in a scenario occur, the decision maker will be able to anticipate how the future will unfold. These trigger events will be seen as information among the stream of data that impacts on the decision maker.

Just as the new purchaser of a particular make of car becomes very sensitive to the number of models of that make on the road, and the differences in levels of equipment, etc., the scenario thinker becomes sensitive to a scenario starting to unfold and becoming reality. Such sensitivity can lead to early contingency action towards an unfavourable future.

Alternatively, new business opportunities can be grasped quickly as soon as favourable scenarios begin to unfold. Such early recognition and reaction to an emerging future is seen by some practitioners as more useful than the creation of robust strategic options.

Typical outcomes of the scenario planning process include:

- confirmation that the business idea is sound, or that new strengths need to be added to create more robustness;
- confirmation that lower-level business choices are sound, or that alternative new options are more robust;
- recognition that none of the business options are robust and therefore contingency planning against unfavourable futures is necessary;
- sensitivity to the early-warning elements that are precursors of desirable and unfavourable futures.

Essentially then, scenario planning downplays managers' poor ability to make valid predictions of the future – an inability that we documented in the previous chapter. Instead, scenario planning is a methodology for developing a range of plausible futures that capture the key uncertainties (as they resolve themselves one way or another) across the range of constructed scenarios.

In this approach, dissenting opinion about the nature of the future is given airtime rather than being suppressed by a growing, but inappropriate, cohesion in the management team as it strives to reach consensus about the nature of the future. As we saw in Chapter 2, groupthink is an unwelcome outcome of cohesion in a management team. The intellectual resources of an organisation are often disparate. Heterogeneity of thought is, in itself, a key resource of an organisation. Scenario planning preserves and cherishes this heterogeneity.

The following four articles illustrate the use of scenario planning at Shell, one of the world's largest corporations.[6] The fifth article in the set describes the work of Peter Shwartz, a pioneer of the scenario planning method and an ex-Shell employee.

'Somewhere over the rainbow', by Anna Smith, *Management (Auckland)*, 1 April 1997 (Copyright UMI company 1997. All Rights Reserved. Copyright Profile Publishing Limited April 1997)

... Shell International's global scenarios present two views of the world's future up to 2020. Both are based on the belief that there is no alternative to adapting to the forces of liberalisation, globalisation and technology. The only question is what sort of society is best able to harness them and therefore succeed.

In the first scenario, dubbed 'just do it', success is dependent on governments getting out of the way of the market, economies being marked out by fast-paced innovation, and individualism being recognised as the key value.

It is a world of hyper-competition, customisation, self-reliance and informal networking. The United States is the model country under this scenario.

The alternative is dubbed 'da wo', or big me, which is taken from a Chinese proverb meaning sacrifice small me to benefit big me.

In this scenario, successful societies are cohesive, governments matter because they provide key elements in the physical and social infrastructure, and successful companies pursue clear, shared long-term strategies. The 21st century belongs to Asia, which becomes the fastest-growing region.

Roger Rainbow, Shell International's vice-president of global business environment, says scenario builders are in the business of stretching people's minds rather than predicting what will happen.

'We try to make people as aware as possible of the uncertainty and unpredictability of the business environment,' he says. 'By looking at a wide range of options you can also sometimes point out what we call an "unscenario" that is almost certain to happen.'

Rainbow cites as an example a series of Russian scenarios Shell put together in 1991. They all pointed to the Russian economy halving in size over three to four years.

He says that, although the company did not foresee the collapse of the Soviet Union, as a result of its post-collapse scenarios it was cautious about its initial move into Russia.

Rainbow says that earlier use of scenario-style thinking could have altered the course of Shell's other public relations crisis in 1995, its plan to scuttle the redundant Brent Spar oil rig in the North Sea. Protests by environmentalists and a Europe-wide boycott by consumers eventually forced the company to abandon its proposals. 'As soon as Greenpeace landed on the platform the situation changed. It was no longer a simple operational issue,' Rainbow says. 'And I would argue, with hindsight, that then would have been the time to stop and reconsider. One lesson we have learnt is if you have a scenario implicit or explicit in your mind and something happens that's outside it, you really should stop and just think about what you're doing … which we later did on the Brent Spar issue.'

Most Shell scenarios project 25 years into the future but, in the case of the world's energy market, the company has developed 'Stories' for the next 100 years.

Controversially, they point to global warming being as big an issue as the Intergovernmental Panel on Climate Change has painted it. Rainbow says the panel's scenario of the world returning to burning coal when oil and gas supplies ran out, and thereby increasing global warming, was not plausible. 'What they're saying is we'll tell our grandchildren, "Sorry boys and girls, although the planet is boiling away, it's time to pick up your picks, put on your hard hats and go down into the mines and dig up all this black stuff that will make it hotter yet."

'That to us as a scenario is just implausible because… if global warming is really happening the last thing you're going to do when oil and gas run out is to start burning coal.'

'Two world views in Shell's 2020 vision', the *Dominion Independent*, 2 October 1996 (Copyright 1996 the *Dominion Independent*)

Shell International's global scenarios present two views of the future up to 2020.

Both are based on the belief that there is no alternative to adapting to the forces of liberalisation, globalisation and technology.

The only question is what sort of society is best able to harness them and so succeed.

In the first scenario, dubbed 'just do it', success comes to those where governments get out of the way of the market, economies are marked out by fast-paced innovation, and individualism is the key value.

Successful companies are able to harness the latest innovations in technology to identify and take advantage of quick-moving opportunities.

It will be a world of hyper-competition, customisation, self-reliance and informal networking. The United States is the exemplar country.

The second option is dubbed 'da wo', or big me, which is taken from a Chinese proverb meaning sacrifice small me to benefit big me.

In this scenario, successful societies are cohesive, governments matter because they provide key elements in the physical and social infrastructure, and successful companies pursue clear, shared long-term strategies.

East Asia becomes the fastest-growing region and the 21st century belongs to Asia.

The two scenarios, according to Shell, are designed as 'plausible and challenging' stories, not forecasts.

'Unlike forecasts, which can sometimes lull us into thinking we can predict the future, scenarios mirror the unpredictable, world-changing events that we must be ready to face even if we cannot know what they will be,' Shell says.

'Scenarios help us to anticipate, by asking "what if" questions, and to recognise and interpret important events and new developments.'

'Shell's seer to spill year 2020 scenarios before IOD conference', *Independent Business Weekly*, 27 September 1996 (Copyright Pauanui Publishing Limited. All rights reserved)

...The world is on the brink of revolutionary change. The collapse of the Soviet Union is but one symptom. Everywhere is the emerging realisation that authoritarian regimes and centrally planned economies don't work.

The French and American revolutions sparked changes in world view. But this time, thanks to modern communications systems, the revolution will be global.

So how will this affect us and how shall we cope?

Roger Rainbow, Shell International's vice-president of global business environment, will present next Tuesday's Institute of Director's conference with at least two different scenarios in a speech entitled New Frontiers or Barricades.

This will be the first time Shell's in-house team of future trends analysts – credited with having predicted the break-up of the Soviet Union – has presented its work to an audience outside the Shell group.

In his first scenario Rainbow will start with the present move towards free trade and, by likely progression, lead us to a harmonious and prosperous year 2020.

Poor countries outstrip the OECD countries growth rates and, with prosperity and education, curb their own birth rates and environmental delinquency. Rich and poor alike recognise their economic, social and environmental interdependence. Some 60% of the world population earns $10,000 to $20,000 a year.

In his second scenario, Rainbow takes the same present situation and, via a no less likely series of events, arrives at a far less attractive year 2020.

Here, the world community sees today's liberalisation not as a challenge, but as a threat. Protectionism wins out over free trade. Rich countries impoverish their own customers – and, eventually, themselves. Some 90% of the world population earns less than $10,000.

The audience will be asked to consider each scenario and assess its impact on New Zealand.

'Management: A glimpse of possible futures: Scenarios force managers to tackle their assumptions' by Tony Jackson, *Financial Times*, 25 August 1997 (Copyright 1997 the *Financial Times*)

Making up stories about the future might seem a curious occupation for grown-up executives. But there was a time, in the 1970s and early 1980s, when scenarios were a familiar part of the planning process. They then fell out of fashion for a while, as did strategic planning overall. Now that strategy is making a comeback, so are scenarios.

In essence, the scenario technique consists of describing a range of possible futures. Let us suppose that the Chinese economy implodes, or that it flourishes: that the internet enriches the telephone companies, or drives them to ruin. What then?

The aim is not to make predictions, but to provide a framework into which subsequent events can be fitted. If executives have thought out the possible outcomes, they should be quicker to react when one of them arrives. As Arie de Geus, former head of planning at Shell, puts it, they can remember the future.

While scenarios have a long history in the armed services, Shell is generally credited with adapting them to business, in response to the first oil shock of 1973. Other oil companies latched on. Since the oil industry undertakes vast single investments such as refineries or petrochemical complexes, scenarios appealed as a form of risk analysis. What would happen if the oil price soared or plummeted? What were the odds of a given host government collapsing, or nationalising the industry?

Then came the reaction. In a recent book, *The Living Company*, Mr de Geus describes how in the 1980s, Shell's senior executives became sceptical. Making up stories, they said, was great fun and good public relations. But how many decisions could be attributed directly to the scenario process? Today, according to Roger Rainbow, Shell's present head of planning, a balance has been struck. The old practice was for the planners to draw up the scenarios and then make presentations to the line managers: as Mr Rainbow puts it, to 'show and tell'.

Over the last 10 years, he says, there has been more emphasis on getting the managers involved. 'The trend has been to get them to bring scenarios into their decision processes,' he says. 'That's actually quite hard, and we've had a few false starts. But we need to help people make decisions on quite focused issues, down to the level of a specific strategy in a given country, or a specific project.

'These days, you don't know who your future competitors will be. That's given scenarios a new lease of life.' Mr Rainbow would not disagree. In the old days, he observes, Shell's scenario work consisted almost entirely of large-scale stories about the world. Now, much of it is quick, one-off studies on issues of technology or markets, in response to demand from Shell executives …

In 1995, the US manufacturer 3M used scenarios to think about the distribution of its office products in Europe. Would very powerful pan-European distributors appear, on the US model? Or would European patterns remain diverse? And how important would electronic commerce become in 3M's markets?

The German electronics group Siemens used scenarios after forming a telecoms alliance early last year. The alliance aimed to develop switches for broadband communications. The scenarios examined the impact of the internet on one big class of customers, the traditional telephone companies. Sceptics would argue that any sensible company will do this kind of forward thinking anyway. But scenario planning, for its proponents, is above all a process: a means of forcing managers to confront their assumptions. James Herman, vice-president of Northeast Consulting, says: 'Senior executives trust the mental model which got them where they are. But if you're in telecoms, computing or media, the danger is that assumptions from past experience no longer apply. So we use scenarios to update the models.' Also, he argues, managers typically work in teams, and they may sometimes have conflicting assumptions without realising it. By thrashing out scenarios together, they can spot the conflicts and, with luck, resolve them ...

'Taking a peek into the future' by Hamish McRae, the *Independent*, 5 September 1995 (Copyright 1995 Newspaper Publishing Plc)

Will technological change continue to go in bursts, with longish periods of relative stability in between, as it seems to have done in the past? Or will it be a continuous, never-ending, helter-skelter process as it seems to be at the moment? ...

The nature and the pace of technological change is one of ... the key points of the GBN scenarios which he outlined. Since it seems to be the principal concern of most business people (principally because if technology continues to race forward at an ever-greater pace it becomes very hard to make money out of it) ... four possibilities. The first two involved two different sorts of the 'burst of progress/pause and lock in' pattern; numbers three and four, benign and malignant versions of continuous change.

The main difference between the first two is how early the 'lock-in' happens. If it is early then frequently the technology is not the best available. For example, the US colour television system, NTSC, is poorer quality than the various European ones, while the VHS standard for video recorders is technically inferior to Sony's rival Betamax. But in the first case the early development of colour TV in the US meant that the country got a worse system than the rest of the world, while the market clout of the VHS producers meant that Sony's system failed to take off. Another example is MS-DOS, but perhaps the best of all is the QWERTY keyboard. This was designed to slow down typists because the arms of the mechanical typewriters tangled up if they were hit too fast, yet more than a century later it still dominates the keyboards of the world.

If, however, the lock-in happens late or the standard develops naturally in the marketplace, then the chances are that the best system will win. The most intriguing example Peter Schwartz cited from the world of TV are the new video standards established not by the conventional television industry but the new software companies. Will our future TV programmes come, not over the airwaves or by cable from the TV company, but down the phone line from a software house?

But even if the lock-in takes place late, scenario two does assume that at some stage there is a pause. And both one and two see standards as something which come down from producers to the marketplace.

The third scenario is one of perpetual transition and where change comes up from the market. The prime example is the internet, unplanned, market-driven, and being used for all sorts of things which never occurred to its original users. The characteristics of this type of change include very rapid growth (as with the internet), and a structure determined by market signals. The principal barrier to the pace of change is the willingness of humans to accept it. But of course we can reject change through the market: we do not have to join the internet if we do not want to. So this form of change, if a bit frightening, is benign: it carries its own checks and balances.

The malign form of very rapid change is also market-driven, but a market which seems to give the wrong signals. This involves social conflict, violence, market volatility, environmental decay and rising insecurity. Leadership is weak or simply irrelevant. And from a commercial point of view, the pace of change makes it simply not possible to make money out of long-term investment. It is a commercial world, too, where downsizing never ends.

Peter Schwartz reckons that most people in the business community would prefer either the first or the second of the four scenarios: they like an element of institutional stability and a society where authority (be it political authority, or commercial authority) is top-down. They would live with the third scenario, that of constant change. And they fear the final one, rising insecurity and chaos …

For Fred McNulty and his worries about the future of cash, a scenario planning exercise with his top management team would seem to be an appropriate response to his dilemma. Even if he is unable to develop a strategy for Autotell that is robust against the range of plausible futures that will be developed in the scenario planning process, he will be sensitised to the occurrence of early trigger events as an unfavourable – or favourable – future begins to unfold. The planning process may also prompt him to develop contingency plans that he can activate at an early stage in response to an unfavourable future.

Key messages

The process of scenario planning can overcome managers' overconfidence in what is seen as the best-guess future. The process of scenario planning provides a structure for thinking, in detail, about the causal logic of how and why particular futures could unfold. The process of constructing these futures enables a management team to gain a shared understanding of the nature of the future facing their organisation. With such an understanding, strategic choice is much more straightforward – choice options can be tested for robustness against the range of plausible scenarios that have been constructed. If no strategic option is found to be robust, then at least you will be sensitive to the occurrence of key events at the beginning of the scenario stories that indicate that a particular scenario is starting to unfold. As we have seen, some of the world's largest corporations use scenario planning to develop and enhance understanding of what the future may hold.

FIVE

Dealing with Decision Dilemmas

Joe Black looked at the options. For five years he had been the CEO of World Knowledge Encyclopaedias. Over each of the five years, the sales of his flagship encyclopaedia set of books had been decreasing. The reason why was unclear – at least to Joe. His management team had met regularly to diagnose and rectify what they saw as the underlying causes of the downturn. More money had been pumped into marketing – especially in those overseas markets where the majority of sales were made. Also, money had been spent on improving the sales training for the direct sales force. These investments had started over three years ago, but the decline in encyclopaedia sales had not been arrested. Joe pondered; he thought especially about the high cost base of research and administrative support within his division of World Books. Without large sales of the encyclopaedia, these costs would look wasteful in World Books' eyes. Comparisons would be done with other, more standard publishing departments and their cost bases if he couldn't continue to show a surplus on the encyclopaedia operation.

In the last two years, Jim had tried to diversify by opening up direct salesforce centres in Beijing and Taiwan. His idea was to use locally based sales support and to customise the encyclopaedias for local markets by research, development and translation at head office. But even this was not working out well. Turnover of the sales force at the new centres was too high, and the research and administrative resource needed to produce customised products was also high.

Joe thought of a new diversification into CD-ROM versions of World Knowledge Encyclopaedias. Around the world, most individuals now had personal computers, and most, he knew, would like the convenience of a CD-ROM encyclopaedia. He could charge a high price for a customised CD-ROM encyclopaedia and, since only a few other publishers were offering electronic encyclopaedias – and then only general-purpose international ones – he would probably make a lot of sales, at least initially. But he recognised that other publishers would eventually follow his lead. He would have two years of clear blue water.

Joe pondered his dilemma. He could no longer continue placing his trust solely in the paper-based encyclopaedia business. But diversification into new markets or products both held risks. He felt like delaying the decision to see if other options emerged. He also felt that World Books should take some responsibility for the difficulties the encyclopaedia division was facing. After all, they had treated the encyclopaedia business as a cash-cow for years and had taken the profits in the fat years. Now in the lean years, this lack of reinvestment was making itself felt. He also felt that the paper-based encyclopaedia business could turn around. After all, they were a reputable publisher and renewed marketing efforts would, surely, eventually pay off. Perhaps the encyclopaedia adverts had not been aggressive enough and the direct sales force were lacking motivation. A continuing focus on getting the quality and customisation message across would surely deliver the required results in the next year. Joe Black stopped pondering these issues and turned to think about the latest dispute between two research staff that had blown up. He knew that he was firefighting, but staff problems couldn't wait.

Was Joe Black's resolution of his decision dilemma rational? Before we study this question, answer the questions in Box 6.

Details of how to score your answers to the questions are given in Appendix C. These questions were developed from Janis and Mann's conflict theory of decision making.[2]

Avoiding difficult decisions

The conflict theory of decision making describes a number of basic ways in which decision makers cope with the threats or opportunities

Box 6 Decision-Making Questionnaire[1]

Instructions: people differ in the way they face up to making difficult, but important, decisions. Please indicate how you make such decisions by ticking those statements that best characterise your style.

1. After making a decision, I am inclined to play down the real value of the alternative I did not choose.
2. My choices are considered carefully.
3. I feel uncomfortable when faced with big decisions.
4. If a decision can be made by me or another person, I often let the other person make it.
5. I try to find out the disadvantages of all alternatives that I am considering.
6. When decisions turn out badly, I tend to put the responsibility on other people.
7. When I have to make a decision, I wait for a long time before getting round to focusing on it fully.
8. When I have a crucial decision to make, I try to forget about it.
9. I try to be clear about what I want to achieve in a decision before I choose.
10. Even after I have come to a decision, it is a while before I act on it.
11. I feel better about choosing if I can convince myself that the decision is not all that important.
12. When making decisions, I prefer to collect as much information as possible.
13. I avoid making major decisions.
14. After I make a decision, I spend a lot of time convincing myself that I have made the best choice.
15. I waste a lot of time on trivial matters before getting to the final decision.
16. I prefer that people who are better informed than me decide for me.
17. I consider carefully how best to make an important decision.
18. Looking back on decisions, I sometimes find that I have overlooked important information.
19. Others should make the big decisions, not I.
20. I don't make decisions unless I really have to.
21. I like to evaluate all of the alternatives in some detail.

22. Whenever I face a difficult decision, I often feel pessimistic about making the best choice.
23. I tend to delay making decisions until it is too late.
24. I don't like to take personal responsibility for major decisions.
25. While coming to a decision, I tend to focus on positive information about my preferred alternative.
26. If I can delay a decision, then I will.

that are often part of crucial decisions. Often, decision makers defensively avoid the stress of difficult decision dilemmas by adopting coping patterns in their decision behaviour. There are three major coping patterns. Procrastination entails delaying the decision, for example waiting for a long time before thinking about the dilemma. Shifting responsibility entails passing the ultimate responsibility for the decision to other individuals or groups. Bolstering involves uncritically boosting the advantages of the least worst option of those options that are available – often the status quo or business-as-usual option. All three coping patterns lower the stress inherent in facing up to a difficult decision. Only vigilant decision making involves the cool, analytical evaluation of options. We have more to say about analytical decision making in Chapters 6 and 7. For now, we focus on how decision makers defensively avoid the stress of difficult decision dilemmas by procrastination, shifting responsibility and bolstering.

Regardless of which of these three defensive avoidance coping patterns are adopted, either singly or in combination, there are two common outcomes – incomplete search for, and evaluation of, incoming information that would aid choice, and lack of contingency planning in the event that the course of action being followed begins to fail badly.

Case study of a management team facing a decision dilemma

In one study I was involved with recently, we interviewed nine individuals on the senior management team of a major corporation who were facing just such a crucial decision dilemma.[3] The current strategic direction was failing, and all alternative strategies were fraught with risk. Essentially, the company had strong core competencies that underpinned its older business idea, but this idea was failing against a changing world – much the same as Joe Black's dilemma. Quotations from our complete interview data – collected from the top management team – were categorised under Janis and Mann's headings.

The following quotations illustrate that the risks were perceived to be serious if the company didn't change its current failing strategy:

> *The business needs more income streams … therefore, diversification is crucial now to build significant other income streams … (participant 1)*

> *A key danger is that there is too much emphasis on our core business activity … New technology could result in the death of [Beta Co.'s main offering] by 2005, 2010, 2015. Who knows when? … We need to move to new areas that will result in new revenue streams … The failure of [Beta Co.] to develop alternative revenue streams would be another bad scenario … (participant 2)*

> *If we go on as we are, in ten years from now we won't be here … (participant 3)*

> *There is a perception round here that [Beta Co.] has very much got all its eggs in one basket. If one of [Beta Co.'s major customers] pulled out … At a personal level, I am very much concerned that we have job security … (participant 5)*

And the risks are also seen to be serious if the company did change strategy:

> *We are a group of talented amateurs rather than experienced in areas of potential diversification … (participant 4)*

[Beta's latest experimental venture] has been a protracted and salutary experience. There are very few short-term gains to be made ... (participant 6)

We are naïve on the business side. [Beta Co.'s latest experimental venture] is necessary for our future but we have had a slightly unrealistic view of how easy or difficult it would be to break into an existing market in which potential customers have settled relationships and [Beta Co.] has no track record ... (participant 7)

The senior management team was also attempting to shift responsibility for its adherence to the current failing strategy to the top-level board of directors, i.e. 'buck-passing':

One main board director is on the record as having said that [Beta Co.] should make no attempt to adapt to changing market conditions ... (participant 1)

The board faces a key decision, not us. They need to take a keen interest in terms of what shape [Beta Co.] should take in the future ... (participant 3)

We have to try and resolve the diversification issue one way or the other, but I am not sure that this is a decision we can take ... (participant 7)

There was also evidence of delay and procrastination:

The failure to diversify would probably mean the business would still be OK in ten years from now, but after 15 years it would be starting to decline ... (participant 1)

There is still mileage in [Beta Co.'s main offering] for the next ten years ... (participant 5)

Things will be slower than most people think ... We are 20 years away from complete change, i.e. our business will still be serviceable in 20 years time ... (participant 6)

There is no real rush to adapt .... Five to ten years away there will still be a healthy market for [Beta Co.'s main offering] ... (participant 7)

Finally, there was evidence of bolstering the current failing strategy:

The slow pace of change in our industry is of benefit to us ... if [Beta Co.] becomes the only [provider of its current main offering] there will be less pressure on us to develop other products ... [Beta Co.'s] current performance and historical record are its key strengths ... (participant 2)

One of the problems we face in respect of new products is customer inertia ... Customers are generally conservative because they don't want the hassle of changing [suppliers]. These same forces are potentially prolonging the life of [Beta Co.'s current main offering] ... (participant 2)

Ultimately, I was brought in [to Beta Co.] to play a key role in enabling the organisation to diversify and/or add to its core business – though diversification may not be needed if [Beta Co.] becomes [the major player within the market of its current main offering] within the next two to three years ... (participant 2)

In short, the current strategy was failing, alternative strategies were perceived to be risky, and buck-passing, procrastination and bolstering were apparent. But what of information search and contingency planning? The following quotations illustrate deficiencies and limitations in these dimensions of strategic thinking. As illustrations of limited information search, consider:

> *I believe you can always buy the skills you need. You may have to pay a bit more or wait a bit … (participant 1)*
>
> *We don't know enough about the real strategic aims of [Beta Co'.s main customers] … (participant 4)*
>
> *We lack understanding of real customer requirements … We know even less about potential customers … (participant 4)*
>
> *There is a learning process we need to go through, but I am sure we can do it and beat the competition … (participant 5).*

As examples of poor contingency planning consider:

> *Currently the business is cash rich but not investing … (participant 1)*
>
> *Another key requirement is for investment in R&D to secure the organisation's future through the creation of new revenue streams, but how should this be done? … (participant 2)*
>
> *I guess we ought to be doing other things to protect ourselves … (participant 5)*
>
> *We lack the ability to talk to the right people in [key alternative sectors]. Are we heavyweight enough? … Our main sources on the [XXXX] side tend to be conferences, suppliers or reading the press … (participant 7)*
>
> *How do we diversify and into what? … (participant 9)*

Dealing with psychological reactions to difficult decisions

The above case analysis illustrates what we believe to be a common organisational reaction to hard-to-make crucial decisions. Figure 4 summarises the conclusions of this chapter, and combines these with the conclusions of Chapters 1, 2 and 3.[4] The diagram represents

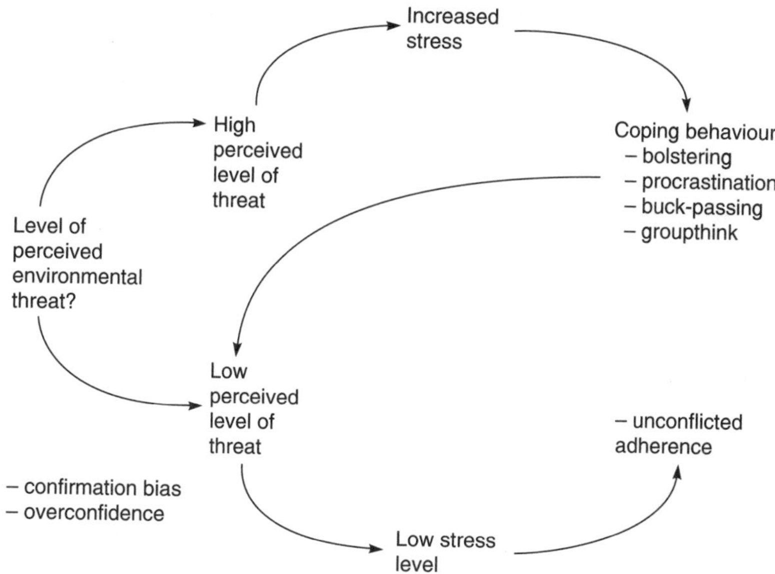

Figure 4 *The relationship between the business environment and the strategic process.*

the relationship between threats in the business environment and the strategic process within the organisation, as a system of dependencies.

In the diagram, the resting state of the system is that of a low perceived level of environmental threat to the organisation's current strategy, which naturally produces little stress in the top management team. Unconflicted adherence to the current strategy characterises this resting state. The case studies of Marks & Spencer and the reaction of Electrolux and Miele to Dyson's new prototype vacuum, which we described in Chapter 1, illustrate habitual adherence to a success formula. Nevertheless, all organisations monitor the business environment for new threats, but this monitoring is degraded by overconfidence and the confirmation bias – both discussed in Chapter 3. These judgemental biases mean that emerging threats to the current success formula are not easily recognised as such.

However, if the threats become so severe that they are finally recognised as threatening the success of the organisation's current strategic direction, and a change of strategy to deal effectively with the threat is not obvious, then the rising organisational stress is reduced by the coping patterns of procrastination, shifting responsibility and bolstering. Additionally, as the current failing strategy is bolstered by the top management team, groupthink processes – described in Chapter 3 – will produce a sense of rightness in, and invulnerability of, the advocated strategy. As we saw in Chapter 3 in our discussion of the space shuttle Challenger incident, in high-consequence situations, dissenting opinion, if raised, is quickly suppressed and the feeling of faith by the top management team in its chosen strategy grows stronger. But, as with the Challenger incident, events in the business environment are not controlled by a cohesive, same-thinking, top management team. Just as a gambler wills the roulette ball to land in the red (even though the roulette ball is not influenced by this willpower), the strategic decision maker's methods of coping with the stress of decision dilemmas will go unrecognised by the course of events already in train. For this reason, we advocate the standard use of scenario planning in any organisation's strategic deliberations since it contains components to promote alternative views about the nature of the future and also challenges what may be inappropriate confidence – both in a single best-guess future and in a single tried-and-trusted strategy. However, in terms of Figure 4, interventions such as scenario planning may be seen by management to be unnecessary, since the increased stress of a misfit between strategy and environment may either (i) have not been experienced because of the dominance of outdated mental frames (Chapter 1), or (ii) have been reduced to tolerable levels by psychological coping mechanisms. In terms of Figure 4, the most appropriate point for a scenario planning intervention in an organisation is theoretically after there is a recognition that the environmental threat to current strategy is high but before the psychological processes inherent in coping behaviour are engaged. However, as yet little is known about whether there is a time delay (and if so how long) between management's recognition of a serious environmental threat to current strategy and the engagement of coping patterns. Janis and Mann's model infers that the engagement and deployment of coping patterns are automatic and subconscious, such that individual managers will not recognise their deployment.

It follows that strategic inertia in the face of environmental threat may be widespread in many organisations – and specific recognition of the usefulness of scenario planning to increase perceived threat and facilitate strategic change in a particular situation may be lost.

For Joe Black and World Knowledge Encyclopaedias, the recommendation is clear-cut: Joe should be aware that his thoughts and actions indicate that he is defensively avoiding his decision dilemma. He and his management team need to think more comprehensively about the threats and opportunities in the business environment – and scenario planning can help him do just that.

Key messages

The lesson from this chapter is that difficult but important decisions are seldom faced head-on. In such situations, managers tend to delay, pass the decision dilemma to others, or psychologically build up the advantages of the least-worst option. These psychological processes reduce the stress engendered by decision dilemmas to tolerable levels. However, such coping behaviour also reduces the quality of the resultant decisions – although the decision maker may not be conscious of this. For this reason, we advocate the use of scenario planning as a standard intervention in any organisation's strategic planning process.

A key point is that you should try to be sensitive to conversations within your organisation that indicate either procrastination, shifting responsibility or bolstering a failing strategy. Such defensive avoidance of difficult decision dilemmas will lead to deficiencies and limitations in information-seeking, and result in poor contingency planning for

SIX

Expectation and Decision Making

Jane Ingle contemplated her decision. On the one hand, she could choose to continue the development of the titanium-braced bike frames. On the other, she could stop this development and continue development of the graphite-based frames. It was either one or the other – but not both. Alternatively, she could choose to stop further development of both products and rely on her current product range of alloy-based frames.

The decision was difficult because neither development was guaranteed to lead to a production-ready design. On the basis of her past experience in bike-frame development, Jane felt that there was a 75% chance that the titanium design could be developed within the year whilst successful development of the graphite design was more problematic and she hazarded a 60% chance of success. If she pursued the titanium design, having failed to complete it within the year, then she felt that the chance of success within a second year was lower, at about 30%. Conversely, successful pursuit of the graphite design was more assured, with prolonged development time, since the technology was less experimental. Jane estimated an 80% chance of success, with continued effort, over the subsequent year.

But the real issue was the pay-offs for each of the alternative strategies. Jane estimated that abandoning both developments now would entail a write-off of about £850 000. Abandoning the titanium development after another year would result in a write-off of £3 million, whereas abandoning the graphite development at the same stage would mean a write-off of £2 million.

If she pursued either of these advanced designs into a second year, then Jane estimated that abandoning at that late stage would mean write-offs of £7 million and £5 million for the titanium and graphite designs, respectively.

On the positive side, though, the outcomes could be bright indeed. If the titanium design was ready for production at the end of the first year, then she estimated that profits would be cumulated to £10 million over five years in net present value terms.

A five-year time horizon seemed appropriate given depreciation and the gradual obsolescence of new innovations. If it took two years, then she estimated cumulative profits at £6 million.

By contrast, success with the graphite-based bike frame development would lead, she guessed, to cumulative profits of £7 million, or £3 million, depending on first- or second-year success, respectively.

Overall, a lot of numbers! But what was the best decision? Stay with the tried and trusted or go for the development of one of the new technologies? A difficult decision and one that Jane was already having sleepless nights about.

Recall that in Chapter 3, we demonstrated overconfidence in management judgements of the likelihood of events such as the ones that Jane Ingle is attempting to predict. For the moment, put your scepticism about the quality of Jane's predictions on hold. We will deal with this apparent contradiction towards the end of this chapter.

Decision trees

One way to help Jane think more deeply about her decision problem is to draw it using a decision tree (Figure 5). Such trees read from left to right. A square is used to represent a decision that the decision maker is facing, and a circle represents a set of events – one of which will definitely happen, but since Jane is not a clairvoyant, there is some uncertainty about which one. At the right-hand side of each of the branches in the decision tree are the pay-offs attached to a particular sequence of decision and events occurring.[1]

The option of continuing development of the titanium bike has a

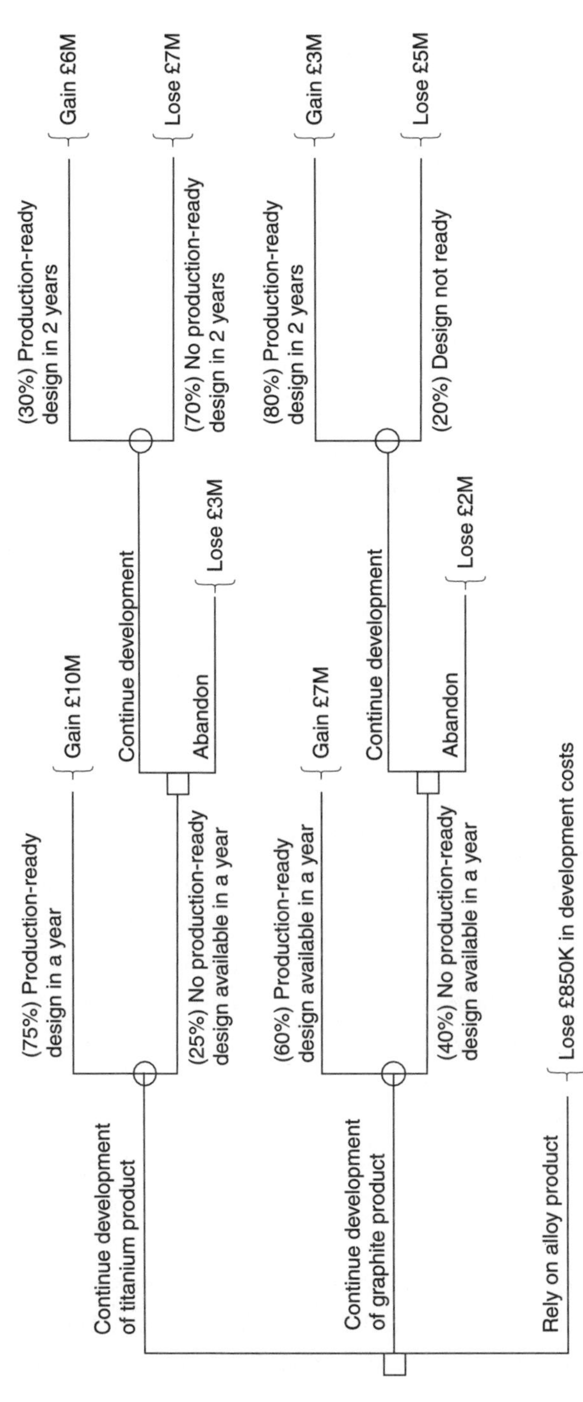

Figure 5 *Decision tree.*

possible payoff of £10 million. If this is not achieved, then there is an option of abandoning at a loss of £3 million. By contrast, continuing development of the graphite bike frame has a possible, but less likely, pay-off of £7 million with an abandonment option costing £2 million.

Of course, Jane could also abandon both possible developments now – at a cost of £850k.

Pessimism

What is the best decision? The risk-averse option would be to abandon now and write off the £850k. Continuation of either development option will lead to an even greater loss if Jane abandons after one year's additional, but unsuccessful, development. Choosing to carry on development after an unsuccessful additional year could lead to even greater losses. Choosing to write off the £850k is called a minimax strategy – if she chooses this, then Jane is choosing to minimise the maximum possible loss. Minimax is a very pessimistic choice strategy in that it assumes that 'bad things always happen to me and I must plan to avoid them'.

Optimism

By contrast, it is possible that continuing development of the titanium-based design would lead to the maximum possible gain of £10 million or, failing that, the third highest maximum of £6 million. If Jane chose to maximise the maximum possible outcome (maximax) then she would choose to continue titanium development. Maximax is an optimistic choice strategy: 'the best outcome could be within my grasp.'

Expectation

A third way of making a decision is to calculate the expectation attached to Jane's three immediate decision options. The expectation attached to continued reliance on the alloy bike frame is clear-cut – a loss of £850k in development costs.

The expectation attached to continued titanium development is a little more complex to calculate. Continuing development for the second year brings with it a 30% chance of a gain of £6 million and a 70% chance of a loss of £7 million. The expectation is thus 30% of +£6 million plus 70% of –£7 million = £1.8 million – £4.9 million = expected loss of £3.1 million. So, at the end of the first year of titanium development, the choice facing Jane is to abandon development and write off £3 million or continue and expect a loss of £3.1 million. If Jane chooses to maximise expected value (i.e. in this case minimise her losses), she would abandon at this point. If we roll back the loss of £3 million, then the expectation of continuing titanium development into the first year carries with it a 75% chance of a gain of £10 million coupled with a 25% chance of a loss of £3 million. Overall, this expectation is £7.5 million – £0.75 million = a positive expectation of £6.75 million.

By contrast, continuing graphite development for a second year carries with it an 80% chance of £3 million coupled with a 20% chance of a loss of £5 million. This works out to an expectation of £2.4 million – £1 million = £1.4 million. Rolling this expectation back along the graphite branch of the decision means that at the end of one year's development, Jane should choose to continue development, with a positive expectation of £1.4 million, rather than abandon at a loss of £2 million. Rolling back further, continuing graphite frame development into the first year carries with it an expectation of a 60% chance of a gain of £7 million coupled with a 40% chance of a gain of £1.4 million. This expectation is £4.2 million + £0.56 million = £4.76 million.

So, in summary, Jane faces three choices:

- Continue with titanium development – expectation of £6.75 million.
- Continue with graphite development – expectation of £4.76 million.
- Abandon both developments and rely on the alloy product – expectation of –£0.85 million.

In terms of the expectation approach, the choice is clear-cut: Jane should continue with titanium development. If she is unable to develop a production-ready design at the end of the first year, then she should abandon this development.

So, Jane now has three rationales for making her decision:

- *Minimax:* recommendation – abandon developments now.
- *Maximax:* recommendation – continue titanium development, if necessary for two years.
- *Expectation:* recommendation – continue titanium development for one year, and then, if unsuccessful, abandon development.

Many managers adopt minimax. Most of us work in organisations where there is a blame culture. If a decision leads to a bad outcome, then the person who made the decision/has the responsibility is to blame. Very few managers are happy with the optimism contained in the maximax strategy.

But minimax is risk avoiding, and organizations who follow this approach will surely minimise their losses but will also minimise their gains. By contrast, the expectation approach will result, if it is applied consistently over a sequence of decisions, on average in higher gains. To see this, consider thought problem 10.

Thought problem 10

You have to pay £1 to take part in a gambling game. This game will result in either a pay-off of £10 or a penalty of £7. The result is based on whether a coin lands heads or tails. Would you take part in the game? If you would, then how many times would you be prepared to take part?

Let's work out the expectation of the gamble. There is a 50% chance of gaining £10 and a 50% chance of losing £7. This expectation is £5 – £3.50 = £1.50. But entry to the game costs £1, and so the overall expectation of each gamble is 50p. With a single play of the game, it is possible that you would lose £8 (£1 entrance fee plus loss of £7), and by the minimax choice principle, you should decline the opportunity to take part, even once. In terms of the maximax strategy, there is a possibility of a win of £9 on each play. A pure maximax strategy would say play the gamble at every opportunity.

But notice that each play of the gamble also gives a positive expectation of 50p. A small amount, but enough for the rational decision maker to also take part at each opportunity. If there are 100 opportunities, then the overall expectation is 100 × 50p = £50. An infinite amount of opportunities would result in an infinite amount of expectation!

In such a situation, the minimax strategy of declining to gamble would clearly be a poor one.

Obviously, such gambling opportunities are fantasy. But if *all* your decisions are made on the same basis – that of maximising expectation – then in the long run your accumulated pay-offs will accumulate in the same way as illustrated in thought problem 10. Consequently, decision making by the expectation approach will outperform minimax. But of course each single decision made by the expectation approach could lead to a poor outcome; in Jane Ingle's case, a loss of £3 million. So a good decision process can, by chance, lead at times to a poor outcome. Organisations whose culture punishes those individuals whose single decision results in a poor outcome are, at the same time, promoting lowered expectations in the long run.

Sensitivity and expectation

But as we saw in Chapter 3, our confidence in our predictions and forecasts can be misplaced – judgement can be overconfident and flawed, especially when there is no frequency or base-rate information available to guide judgement. Fortunately, the expectation approach has been developed to analyse the degree to which estimates of probabilities or pay-offs have to change in order to switch the decision from the recommended one to another of the options. Look back at the decision tree in Figure 5. If, for example, Jane's probability estimate of a 75% chance of the titanium design being fully developed in a year is lowered to 50%, then the expectation of this branch of the tree is also lowered to £3.5 million (50% of £10 million – 50% of £3 million). This expectation is less than the £4.76 million expectation of continuing the graphite bike frame development.

In fact, if the 75% chance drops to 60%, then the expectations of the graphite or titanium development options are very nearly equal. The key question that Jane must ask herself is: are the chances of a production-ready titanium design being available after one year's development greater than 60%? If she is sure that they are, then further sensitivity questions can be developed from the decision tree and expectation calculations. It may well be that the decision is insensitive, except for implausibly large changes in estimates of probabilities and pay-offs. By contrast, if the decision is sensitive in some of its components, then more information can be gathered to both support and challenge these estimates. The advice for Jane Ingle? Given that extensive sensitivity analysis reveals little or no sensitivity to reasonable changes in her estimates of probabilities and pay-offs, then she should follow the expectation approach and continue titanium development for one year and then, if unsuccessful, abandon development. If, by contrast, some of Jane's estimates are sensitive, then she should seek to challenge them by seeking disconfirming information – as we described in Chapter 3.

If a management team is involved with the decision, then a similar approach can be used to see whether differences in estimates between members of the team have any significant impact on the recommended decision. For example, in Jane's case, estimates of 65% or above would have no impact: titanium development would be supported.

Key messages

The construction of decision trees can help crystallise complex decisions that have several stages nested within one another. If you feel that pay-offs for the possible outcomes of the decision can be estimated, *and* that probabilities can be assessed for the events portrayed in the tree, then the expectation approach can be applied to identify the best decision option. As we have seen, in the long run, adopting the expectation approach will result in the accumulation of a larger amount of pay-off than choosing by either minimax or maximax. However, the expectation approach can, within a single decision, result in a poor pay-off – one that would have been avoided by choosing, pessimistically, on the basis of minimax.

We now move on to discuss the consequences of a blame culture in organisations. What happens when a decision does result in a poor outcome? What is the responsible decision maker's likely reaction?

Blame culture and risk taking

Jim Prior felt bad. He had spent the whole of last week looking through the progress reports, and it was clear that there hadn't been much. The division was behind the target that he had set them. He knew that the main board would call a halt once they found out. It was clear-cut – continuing investment would be best placed in other divisions and on other projects. But he felt bad. He felt bad because the whole enterprise was down to him. The original conception had been his idea. He had convinced the main board to invest and he, personally, had hand-picked the team leader and most of the team. In the first year, progress had been good and his bonus last year had been based, in the main, on the early success. But the picture had changed – and how! He had to turn the project around. Personnel changes would have some effect, but the key was increased investment in both plant and materials. Without it there was no chance of success. Jim thought hard. There was money he could 'borrow' for about nine months. It was simply a matter of delaying the introduction of the new automated plant control system. He had the money in his budget. He could move it between headings – at least in the short term. In nine months' time, he would have to think again. But by that time he knew the project would be back on target.

In several studies conducted in Staw and Ross's laboratory, this 'escalation of commitment' phenomena has been investigated in detail.[2] The basic approach has been this: individual respondents – usually MBA students – are asked to allocate R&D funds to one of two operating divisions of a company. The company and the decision context are described in detail, and the respondent is then told that after a year the investment had either proved successful or unsuccessful and that he/she is now faced with a second decision concerning a second allocation of funds. This part of the experiment is called the 'high-responsibility condition'. Individuals in a second group (labelled the 'low-responsibility condition') were told that another financial officer of the firm had made the earlier decision and that it had been either successful or unsuccessful. These individuals were then asked to consider making a second allocation of funds to the division.

When the outcome of the earlier decision proved to be an unsuccessful investment, the high-responsibility MBAs allocated significantly more funds to the operating division that they had originally chosen than the low-responsibility MBAs. By contrast, the allocation decisions made by both groups of MBAs were roughly the same *if* the earlier decision had produced a successful outcome.

As W.C. Fields once said, 'If at first you don't succeed, try, try again. Then quit. No use in being a damn fool about it.'

What were the common elements of Jim Prior's decision and that of the high-responsibility MBAs? First, there was a second decision to make as a result of a previous unsuccessful decision. Second, there was a degree of personal responsibility and subsequent disappointment felt for the poor consequences of the important prior decision.

In such situations, before committing funds to the second of what may be a series of linked decisions, managers pay more attention to information that confirms the validity of their earlier decision – recall the confirmation bias discussed in Chapter 3. Also, since the second decision is made in a situation that is negatively framed – recall our analysis of decision making in the domain of losses described in Chapter 1 – then individuals will tend to select risk-seeking options that potentially can recover what has become an adverse situation. Also, of course, a blame culture within an organisation will magnify the likelihood that failure will be concealed or ensure that additional effort is made to turn the situation around – hence Jim Prior's resolution of his particular dilemma at the start of this section.

How can an organisation halt such 'non-rational escalation of commitment'? The key point is that organisations should evaluate managers on the basis of good decision processes rather than good outcomes. Good decisions carry the risk of poor outcomes. Managers should be allowed to reverse decisions if they begin to fail.

But, as the following articles show, reversing a decision is not that easy. The first article analyses the Taurus computer project in the City of London. The next four articles document Nick Leeson's downfall as a currency trader at Baring's Bank in Singapore. The final four articles provide insight into the funding of the Millennium Dome project in London.

'Technology: sudden death of a runaway bull – the Taurus project was blighted by misjudgement, mismanagement and neglect' by Richard Waters and Alan Cane, *Financial Times*, 19 March 1993 (Copyright 1993 the *Financial Times*)

It was a form of collective madness. The City's biggest computer project, Taurus, cost hundreds of millions of pounds and kept computer departments in the financial industry busy for years. But just a week after it was killed off, no one in the city can think of any good reasons why it was being built at all.

'It was a case of widespread myopia,' says one senior banker with a close involvement in the Taurus project.

'We should have stood back more and taken a broader look,' says Patrick Mitford-Slade, chairman of the committee that devised the system. A London Stock Exchange executive close to the project adds that the 'uncritical acceptance of received wisdom' throughout the securities industry meant that, once started, the project acquired a life of its own ... Extensive interviews with people close to the Taurus project reveal a sequence of misjudgement, mismanagement and neglect ... Most of the people closely associated with the system's conception admit to fundamental errors of judgement.

The full extent of the problems became clear to the stock exchange's board only last week – five years after the project started in earnest and more than a decade since it was first proposed ... 'There were no redeeming features,' one computer specialist said, pointing out that the exchange had broken virtually every rule of computer project management during the five-year span of the project ... A big error, in retrospect, was the decision to use as the heart of the new software a computer package developed by Vista Concepts of New York ... The problems were compounded by the constant redefining of the project requirements. The exchange paid £1 million for the Vista package. Revisions to it were projected to cost a further £4 million, but by the end the software had cost £14 million and had still not been completed ... The heads of computer departments across the City were deeply embroiled in Taurus – and many moaned continually about the project – but few, if any, ever called for a big rethink. 'Nobody was brave enough to stand up and say, this doesn't make sense,' says a member of the Taurus monitoring group ...

A series of management consultancy firms pored over the project, though none expressed serious reservations until recently. Touche Ross had been brought in as a monitor for the project at the outset and helped to produce the cost estimates used to justify the project. Its role was ended by Rawlins in 1990, who decided that the job done by the external monitors could equally well be done by the exchange's management.

Coopers & Lybrand supplied 18 staff on secondment to the project, led by Watson. In the summer of 1991, when the concern of senior exchange management was first aroused, a Coopers consultant was asked to complete a review of the project. His advice: that Taurus could still be completed, with some management changes.

Senior partner Brandon Gough was also involved in discussions with the exchange at that time – although Coopers now says that it never had any direct involvement in the project, but was simply supplying consultants to work under exchange supervision ...

Concerns were first reported by an *outside* [my italics] consultancy firm last autumn, when Andersen Consulting – which would eventually have been required to run the settlements system – was asked to review the project. It was this review that revealed that there was no overall architecture for the Taurus system ...

When the recriminations have died down, the City will still be left with the same problem it faced in the early 1980s: how to build a modern stock market settlement system ...

'High-flyer who lost his Barings. It was difficult to believe that the gambling instinct of a young man from Watford could bring down one of the City's blue-blooded institutions – but Nick Leeson's trades managed precisely that' by Lary Elliott with Patrick Donovan, Sarah Whitebloom, Lawrence Donegan in Malaysia and Pauline Springett in Singapore, the *Guardian*, 3 April 1995 (Copyright 1995 the *Guardian*)

... For the moment, nobody really knows what was racing through Nick Leeson's mind as he hurriedly threw clothes into a couple of suitcases in his luxury Singapore condominium nine days ago.

Such revelations will, presumably, have to wait for the memoirs of the man who in seven days had brought down Britain's oldest merchant bank ... The last, frantically scribbled note he left, saying he was sorry for the financial black hole he had created in the Barings accounts, suggests the pressure that had been mounting since the turn of the year had simply become too intense ... A London-based bank was losing money on the Tokyo stock market as a result of the activities of a 'rogue' trader in Singapore, who then fled to Kuala Lumpur, northern Malaysia, and oil-rich Brunei before flying back to face the music in Frankfurt. No question, the Leeson story has style. Then there is the scale of the losses, £500 million at the weekend, £700 million on Monday after a 4 per cent fall in the Tokyo stock market triggered by the weekend revelations. To those uninitiated in the rituals of the derivatives market it beggared belief that one man could expose his bank to such losses ... These losses mounted so catastrophically that by last Friday morning at a crisis meeting, the bank directors learnt that Barings had been rendered effectively bankrupt by liabilities which then stood at £500 million. These are the bald facts. As investigators across the globe start unravelling the threads of the most sensational scam in the history of the City, it is clear that nobody yet knows how this was allowed to happen – or, indeed, has deduced the motives behind Mr Leeson's trades. One of the biggest puzzles is why Mr Leeson continued piling up his exposure to trades on the Osaka Stock Exchange after the January 17 Kobe earthquake sent share prices reeling.

The Bank of England disclosed earlier this week that on or around January 26 – when the Japanese markets were falling rapidly – Mr Leeson started building up his position in a flurry of share deals. The result was to accumulate a potential exposure of £17 billion.

This is the heart of the Baring affair. Mr Leeson would have been fully aware, as soon as the markets reacted to the Kobe earthquake, that he faced heavy losses. So did he panic? Was he trying to trade himself out of a hole on the desperate assumption that the Osaka market would soon rally before his losses became apparent? …

Mr Leeson may have been attempting to recoup his losses by doubling and then redoubling his stake … Market insiders find it hard to credit that no one at Barings was aware of Mr Leeson's activities. It has emerged this week that senior executives in London had authorised the advance of large sums of money to the 'rogue trader' at the end of January in order to support his activities … Throughout February, he continued to request further cash as the bank's position became more and more precarious and the margin calls mounted. Barings insiders claim that head office thought the risks were hedged – despite growing disquiet throughout the organisation … The eventual discovery that something was seriously wrong in Singapore is understood to have been made by accident. It is believed that Peter Norris, the head of investment banking at Barings and the man who finally stumbled across the problem, had gone to Singapore about two weeks ago in order to congratulate Mr Leeson on his contribution to Barings' 1994 profits. There was even talk of a seven-figure bonus for the trader. When it met last week, the bank's board was still delighted that the stream of cash coming out of Singapore's futures operations had proved a big plus for Barings' overall profitability. But Mr Norris decided to inquire more closely into the trader's methods. By Thursday, February 23, Mr Norris had been told that something was wrong. By then Mr Leeson had disappeared. The penny dropped. People started asking questions that apparently had never been asked before, or had not elicited the right answers. Realising the extent of the crisis facing the bank, Mr Norris had only one option. It was

7.15am on February 24 when the phone rang at Peter Baring's home. Within the hour, the chairman had gathered the top brass at Barings' Bishopsgate headquarters. The details were sketchy but it was agreed that the Bank of England must be informed.

'Barings like "Mad Hatter's tea party"' by Glenda Cooper, the *Independent*, 6 August 1996 (Copyright 1996 Newspaper Publishing Plc)

Senior managers at Barings knew for more than 18 months that Nick Leeson was running up big losses, according to the bank's former chief executive. They did nothing because they were blinded by the staggering profits he appeared to be making. The result, according to Peter Norris, was a 'Mad Hatter's tea party'.

Mr Norris, who is due to be questioned by the Treasury Select Committee on Monday, has spoken for the first time about the meetings held inside the bank to discuss Leeson, whose trading on the Singapore market (Simex) led to the collapse of Britain's oldest merchant bank with losses of £830 million. In a BBC *Inside Story* documentary to be shown next week, Mr Norris, who was not told about the problems, describes such meetings as 'bizarre'. 'In retrospect one has to admit virtually everything about that discussion was absolutely mad,' he said. 'We were living in a world through the looking glass where logic was apparent but was completely perverted. It seems completely bizarre that a group of rational, intelligent, experienced, competent people were dealing with this matter in a way totally at variance with reality.' Since 1992 Nick Leeson had been covering up his losses on Simex by concealing them in a secret account known as 88888. As his losses mounted he increasingly asked the London office to send him more money for downpayments on futures bought for fictitious clients. The bank complied – sending £700 million by the time he finished trading. From September 1993, managers noticed that there was a discrepancy in Leeson's demands for money and the clients he was supposedly buying for. 'There was clearly an appreciation of the seriousness of what had happened because there was a history of concern in this area,'

Mr Norris said. 'Basically it wasn't acted upon until January, February 1995 which was much too late.' Mr Norris, who has been banned by the Securities and Futures Authority (SFA) from working in the City for three years and fined £10 000, says that he was never told by senior managers about the losses. Instead, managers were blinded by Leeson's fictitious profits – once £10 million in one week. 'Critical faculties were less engaged than they might have been . . . because there were profits,' Mr Norris said.

Ron Baker, the former head of financial products group at Barings International Bank between 1993 and 1995, agrees: 'People sent in to fix the controls were seduced by the commercial success and lost their way...'

'Barings resembled "Mad Hatter's tea party"' by Robert Miller, *The Times*, 7 July 1996 (Copyright Times Newspapers Ltd., 1996)

... Mr Norris, who will be quizzed on his role by the Commons Treasury Select Committee next Monday, told the programme, due to be screened next Wednesday, that at a meeting on January 24 last year the Singapore position was discussed and a committee concluded that Barings was 'doing rather well'. Now he admits ... 'that we were living in a world through the looking glass where logic was apparent, but was actually completely perverted'. The former Barings director continued: 'It seems completely bizarre that a group of rational, intelligent, experienced and confident people were dealing with a matter that was totally at variance with reality . . . Critical faculties were less enjoined than they might have been to put it at its least because there were profits.'

Leeson, who was interviewed for the programme before he left his German prison cell for a 6½-year term in Singapore, variously described the Barings management as 'bumbling fools' and 'idiots'. Mr Norris in turn described Leeson's ability to manipulate people. He said: 'He's like a virus that gets into the workings of something that works, and perverts it utterly. He's an agent of destruction.' Of the audit in the Singapore office in the summer of 1994, Leeson said he 'expected everything to be found'. But, he said: 'They came in and they didn't take any records. So I can't be happier. They didn't test one record or one report. I mean that's not an audit...'

'Britain – inside Blair's big tent: thumbs down for the Dome: more than half the British public think it was wrong to build the Millennium Dome. Will this damage the government?' from the *Economist*, 8 January 2000 (Copyright © 2000 the *Economist*; Source: World Reporter™ – FT McCarthy)

The Millennium Dome was always intended to be a symbol. Tony Blair says that it is meant to 'show Britain as a country confident about the future'. The prime minister's critics have suggested that it is actually a metaphor for the whole New Labour project: a large, grandiose exterior was commissioned, and only afterwards did anyone think about what to put inside it ... A MORI poll commissioned for the *Economist* this week shows that the British public seem underwhelmed: 56% of respondents thought the dome should never have been built; only 38% were prepared to pronounce it a success; and fewer than 40% of those asked agreed with Mr Blair's assertion that the millennium evening celebrations in Britain displayed a new sense of 'confidence and optimism'. If the dome was meant to generate a 'feel-good' factor, it seems – so far – to have failed.

Part of the problem is that the dome was over-sold from the beginning. Mr Blair declared that it would be 'the greatest show on earth'. It would enter the history books alongside the Great Exhibition of 1851, which heralded the industrialisation of Britain, and the Festival of Britain of 1951, which captured the mood of national revival after the second world war. On millennium eve, the prime minister had predicted, the eyes of the world would be on London. Greenwich, the site of the dome, was proclaimed as 'the home of time' and therefore the natural focus for the world's celebrations. The biggest and best fireworks demonstrations in the world would be along the banks of the Thames ... Mr Blair has nailed his colours firmly to the dome's (dozen) masts ...

'Millennium Dome is a disaster, says Short' by Tom Baldwin and Greg Hurst, *The Times*, 22 September 2000 (Copyright Times Newspapers Ltd., 2000)

Clare Short last night admitted that the Millennium Dome was a 'disaster' that should never have been built.

The International Development Secretary's comments will infuriate ministerial colleagues who have continued to defend the loss-making Greenwich attraction despite the Millennium Commission repeatedly having to bail it out with more than £600 million of public money ...

'The black hole of Greenwich: The Millennium Dome's dire difficulties', the *Economist*, 9 September 2000 (Copyright © 2000 the *Economist*; Source: World Reporter™ – FT McCarthy).

Shortly before the Millennium Dome opened in Greenwich at the turn of the year, Tony Blair dismissed the project's critics as cynics who 'despised anything modern and are made uneasy by success'. The Dome's contents, he insisted, would be 'the greatest show on earth'.

These days the prime minister prefers not to talk about the Dome much. That task is left to his hapless friend and Dome minister, Lord Falconer, who on September 5 had the excruciating task of having to defend an extra £47 million ($68 million) subsidy for the Dome, to enable it to keep going before its scheduled closure at the end of the year. This is the fifth emergency cash injection the Dome has received in less than a year. The latest handout brings the amount of lottery money swallowed by the Greenwich tent to £628 million. The basic problem is that the Dome has proved to be much less of an attraction than its promoters expected. Its operators, the New Millennium Experience Company, had originally budgeted on attracting 12 million paying visitors over the course of the year. The company is now expecting just 4.5 million paying visitors during 2000; that works out as a public subsidy of £138 per visitor.

Each new dollop of public money has hitherto been announced with an assurance that this will positively, definitely, be the last time the Dome has to be bailed out ...

'Tell us what went wrong. There was a huge wave of optimism that greeted the dawning of the Year 2000 and many were prepared to give the controversial £670 million Millennium Dome to be opened for just 12 months the benefit of the doubt', ***Leicester Mercury*****, 6 September 2000 (Copyright © 2000** ***Leicester Mercury*****; Source: World Reporter™)**

... There was a huge wave of optimism that greeted the dawning of the Year 2000 and many were prepared to give the controversial £670 million Millennium Dome to be opened for just 12 months the benefit of the doubt. But in the last year the cash needed to keep the attraction open has grown and grown. A £60 million grant in February, £29 million in May, a £43 million advance on the sale of the site in August and now a further £47 million to keep it open until the end of the year ... But the Dome was doomed even before it opened its doors because of wildly inflated projections of how many people it would attract. It has not reached anywhere near that level and good money is being thrown after bad to save face ... There needs to be a full and open inquiry into why the Dome has gone belly up and turned into a bottomless pit for public money.

'The Dome: They haven't got a leg to stand on. It was supposed to symbolise all that was best about Britain in the 21st century. Instead the Millennium Dome has turned into a disaster' by Walter Ellis, the ***Independent*****, 28 May 2000 (Copyright 2000 Newspaper Publishing Plc)**

... When Sir John Bourn, head of the National Audit Office, announced on Wednesday that he intended to open a formal investigation into a possible misuse of funds by the Dome authorities, few were surprised. So much money has disappeared into the Dome – £897 million at the last count – that it has been compared to a financial black hole, from which nothing, not even light entertainment, can escape ...

The Government is under mounting pressure to call a halt. Last week, the Millennium Commission doled out a further £29 million to keep the show on the road. The money, allegedly a final, final tranche, was a 'loan', to be repaid out of profits. Where the profit is to come from remains a mystery ...

At Prime Minister's Questions in the Commons, John Prescott, standing in for Mr Blair, declared pugnaciously that 'nearly six million people' had already visited the Dome. 'That is a huge amount of people.' Sadly for the Deputy PM, he was reading the revised projections for the year as a whole, thus exaggerating the numbers by a factor of 100 per cent. But Mr Prescott's gaffe was not his first in relation to the Dome.

According to Peter Mandelson, Prescott was asked for his opinions at the end of a 1997 Cabinet committee meeting called to decide whether to go ahead with the Dome. Without blinking, he said the Government had to proceed. Otherwise they would be accused of losing their nerve. Having welcomed the imprimatur of his deputy, Blair promptly disappeared to keep an urgent church appointment, leaving Prescott to chair the Cabinet.

And advice for Jim Prior? Jim should be aware that his thoughts and actions indicate that he is falling into the escalation of commitment trap. For Jim's superiors, the advice is clear-cut: make sure that you rotate those individuals who make project review decisions to ensure that those who are responsible for continuation decisions are different people from those who were responsible for earlier commitments.

SEVEN

How to Make Trade-offs

John Bull reviewed the job applicants after the interviews. Jack had the qualifications and references but not the in-depth experience. Jim had the right personality – which meant he would fit easily with the other members of the management team. Moreover, he was high on the qualification side but his reference had been a little ambiguous. Still, he had had useful experience – if his CV could be believed. Jill, on the other hand, was more of a long shot – she had worked in a different industry but was young, bright and seemed ready to learn new approaches. Trouble is she might be too bright – too ambitious and pushy – and would unsettle the current team. The final candidate was Brian. He had been in the industry some eight years. He seemed easy-going and had shown a good knowledge of, and an interest in, his potential new employer. His reference was OK – he had learnt on the job rather than at a business school.

John pondered his decision for a moment. It had to be Brian: he had the experience, would fit in and was interested in the position. Moreover, his interview performance had been good.

How do you feel about the above decision process? Was it soundly based? Most executives, when faced with such a description of a decision, feel that John's choice was too intuitive. Clearly, John had identified what he considered important attributes in the decision: qualifications, industry experience, organisational fit, CV, wider experience, intelligence, age, ambition, pushiness, believability, references, interest in the potential new employer, and interview performance. But he had not been very systematic in working out the importance of these factors for the job-hire decision. Indeed, he had not been very careful in evaluating each of the job candidates on these factors.

We will return to John Bull's decision problem shortly. First, though, consider thought problem 11.

> ***Thought problem 11***
>
> Imagine you have about £6000 to spend and you must purchase a new vehicle this weekend since your current car has just failed its MOT. Every weekday, you have to drive to work, which is 30 miles away. There are hundreds of cars on offer in the local paper, so first you eliminate all those over £6000 and all those less than about £5000. Since you have two small children, all two-seater sport cars are also removed from the choice set. This leaves about 70 cars. Your journey to work each day on a major highway is tedious, but less so if you drive at a high speed. You decide that you want a car with some power and comfort. Accordingly, all cars with engines of less than 1600cc are eliminated. This leaves about 40 cars. Reliability is also important to you and you recall a recent survey that put Japanese and German cars in the top bracket. You focus on the 15 cars that are Japanese or German in manufacture. Some of the car descriptions contain details of the mileage that the car has covered. You reason that as your own average mileage is 20 000 a year, then if the car is to last you for four years it should not have more than 30 000 miles on the clock. This reduces the choice set to 10 cars. You phone round the sellers of these remaining cars and find that only eight of the cars have a full service history, and four of these are painted in awful colours. You put down the phone and drive round to see the four remaining cars, two of which are in dealers' showrooms and the remaining two are for sale privately. One of the private sellers looks suspicious to you. You feel that they may have reduced the mileage recorded on the car's mileometer. Reflecting on this, you focus on the dealers' cars. One of them offers you an excellent price for your current car. You accept their offer and drive away in a metallic grey Toyota with an 1800cc engine and electric sunroof.
>
> Do you consider this to be a good procedure for making the decision?

Simplifying choices can result in poor decisions

When I have presented thought problem 11 on decision-making courses for executives, most say that they do consider the process to be a reasonable one (although there is often some debate on whether the correct attributes were used to make the decision). After all, you cannot give equal consideration to all of the cars, and it makes sense, for example, to make an initial selection of 70 based on price.

Tversky[1] called this process 'elimination by aspects' (EBA). As we have seen, a decision maker using EBA first identifies the most important attribute (in our case, price). Next, a cut-off value (or values) is set for the attribute, and any option failing to meet this cut-off value is eliminated. The decision maker then repeats this process for the second most important attribute, and continues until only one alternative is left.

Clearly, EBA is easy to apply, and is easy to explain and justify to others. In short, the choice process is well suited to busy managers. However, our tendency to choose by EBA can be prone to manipulation by other people. The following television commercial demonstrates this problem:

> *There are more than two dozen companies in the San Francisco area which offer training in computer programming.'*
>
> *[The announcer puts some two dozen eggs and one walnut on the table to represent the alternatives, and continues.]*
>
> *'Let us examine the facts. How many of these schools have on-line computer facilities for training?'*
>
> *[The announcer removes several eggs, which correspond to those schools that do not have this feature.]*
>
> *'How many of these schools are approved for veterans' benefit?' [This classic example is from the time of the Vietnam war and 'veterans' benefit' was paid for participation in courses that were rated as approved by the US Educational Authorities.]*
>
> *[More eggs are then removed and this process continues until the walnut alone remains. The announcer cracks the nutshell, which reveals the name of the company, and concludes.]*
>
> *'This is all you need to know in a nutshell.'*

It follows that decisions made by EBA may be poor because for virtually any available choice alternative, no matter how inadequate it may be, it is possible to devise a sequence of selected aspects (or, equivalently, describe a particular state of mind) that leads to the choice of that alternative. Notice that poor performance on one attribute is not compensated for by good performance on other attributes. In thought problem 11, one of the cars might have been rejected because it was slightly below the 1600cc cut-off value. Yet its price, reliability and mileage may all have been preferable to the car purchased. These strengths could have more than compensated for this one weakness.

EBA is one approach that we use to simplify our choices in complex situations. But other, less complex ways of making choices have been identified by psychologists. Sometimes, we simply focus on what we see as the most important attribute and then select the alternative that is considered to be best on that attribute. For example, in a choice between several tariff/brand packages of mobile phones, a consumer may consider peak-time call costs to be the most important attribute and therefore choose the cheapest package on this attribute. Thus, the choice is made without reference to any other features of the alternative packages, such as line rental, reputation for reliability, or European coverage. In the event of a 'tie' on the most important attribute, the decision maker will choose the option that performs best on the second most important attribute, and so on. Such a decision strategy is simple if there are a few ties. However, such a decision will usually be based on only a small part of the information that is available. For example, when you go shopping you might adopt the following decision strategy: if the price difference between brands is less than 50 pence, choose the higher-quality product; otherwise choose the cheaper brand. Consider the choice between the following prices and perceived quality of standard packs of washing powder. Imagine that you pick up the packs in sequence from a supermarket shelf as you walk down the aisle:

Brand	Price	Quality
A	£3.00	Low
B	£3.30	Average
C	£3.60	High
D	£3.50	Medium

If you were to choose between brands A and B using the above decision strategy, then you would choose brand B. If you were to choose between brands B and C you would choose brand C. Finally, if you were to choose between brands C and D, then you would retain brand C. However, if you were to choose between brand A and brand C you would choose brand A. It follows that using what appears to be a sensible decision strategy results in B being preferred to A and C being preferred to B. This would imply that C is preferred to A but in fact A is preferred to C. This set of choices is irrational in that it contains inherent contradictions. Such irrationality is characteristic of our everyday choices.

There are various reasons that may give rise to such irrational preferences. It may be that the choice between different pairs of alternatives causes you to focus on different attributes. For example, imagine that you are in the process of choosing whether to spend £15 on a theatre ticket, a music CD or a business text. In comparing the theatre ticket and the CD, you may think about a one-off experience of the theatre and choose the CD because it will give repeatable pleasure. Thinking about the CD and the business text, you may choose the text because it may further your career. Finally, when faced with a choice between the theatre ticket and the text, you select the theatre ticket because it will give you a break from your work. Focusing on pairs of options may cause you to concentrate on different attributes – changing the importance you accord to each attribute at each comparison. However, in choosing between the three options it seems intuitively necessary to maintain a consistent view about which attribute is most important.

Satisficing

The strategies we have outlined so far are descriptions of how people make a decision when they are faced with an immediate choice between alternatives that have several attributes of value. Imagine next that you are looking for a new house. You might, over a period of weeks, view several houses as they become available on the market. Herbert Simon, the Nobel Prize-winning economist, has argued that, in these circumstances, decision makers use an approach called 'satisficing'.[2] The key aspect of satisficing is the aspiration level of the decision maker which characterises whether a choice alternative is acceptable or not. Imagine that your aspiration level is a job in a particular geographical location with salary above a particular level and at least three weeks' paid holiday per year. Simon argues that you will search for jobs until you find one that meets your aspiration levels on all these attributes. Once you have found such a job you will take it and, at least for the time being, conclude your job search. Consider also the decision problem of selling your home. Offers for purchase are received sequentially and remain active for only a limited period of time. If you do not accept an offer within a short period of it being made, then the prospective purchaser may follow up other possibilities. Consider purchasing a used car. Cars are on show in many different showrooms scattered across town, and advertisements for private sales appear in the local newspaper every night. Should you look at each car?

How would you solve these decision problems? Herbert Simon would argue that in the house sale example you would wait until you received a 'satisfactory' offer.

Similarly, in the car purchase example, you would continue looking until you found a car that is 'satisfactory' to you. Simon says:

> *In a satisficing model, search terminates when the best offer exceeds an aspiration level that itself adjusts gradually to the value of the offers so far received ... the important thing about search and satisficing theory is that it shows how choice could actually be made with reasonable amounts of calculation, and using very incomplete information.*

In the job search problem, if you are offered and accept a 'satisfactory' job, it is still possible that you might have found a better job if you had been willing to make further job applications and go for further interviews. It is also possible that when you started the job search process, your expectations were unreasonably high such that you might at an early stage delay accepting, or even refuse, what objectively might be an excellent job. A subsequent unsuccessful job search may lower your aspiration level such that you fall back on what is now seen as an acceptable alternative, or you may be forced to accept a job offer that is less desirable than a job you refused earlier as unsatisfactory. Note that in the job search example, there were no considerations of how much holiday you would be prepared to give up for a given increase in salary, i.e. no trade-offs. The final choice also depends on the order in which the alternatives present themselves. If you are searching for a car to buy, then the car you choose will probably be different if you decide to change the order in which you visit the showrooms.

Studies of choice

So far, we have outlined possible choice strategies that people might follow. Next, we describe studies that have attempted to find out which of the above decision strategies is the most general description of how we make choices. One of the most used ways to investigate how people make choices has been the information board, which displays information in the following manner:

	Attributed			
	Cost	Reliability	Miles per gallon	Depreciation
Car A				
Car B				
Car C				
Car D				
Car E				
Car F				

In the early studies with the information board, the board was placed physically in front of the decision maker and the decision maker was able to reveal information to aid his or her choice by lifting, one at a time, any or all of the 24 covers on the board. As the decision maker collects information to make a decision, the researcher can record the sequence of information gathering and gain insight into the type of decision strategy (or strategies) being followed, i.e. *process tracing*. Such information boards have now been superseded by mouse-controlled computer displays. Alternatively, other investigators have presented all information on an 'uncovered' information board and monitored the sequence by which the decision maker attends to the information by following the decision maker's eye movements as he or she looks at the information, rather than monitoring the order in which pieces of information were uncovered.[3]

Information board techniques have revealed that the more attributes and alternatives there are in a decision problem, the smaller the percentage of attributes that decision makers considered. Also, the format in which the information is presented strongly affects the decision maker's search through the information, increasing either search on the attribute scores within an alternative or on an attribute's scores across alternatives.

Time pressure

In one study, Svenson and Edland found that when choices between multi-attributed alternatives were made under increasing time pressure (i.e. the need for a quick choice), then differences in the decision processes between such forced choice and situations in which there was no time pressure became pronounced.[4] This effect was so strong that one type of alternative was preferred under time pressure and another type of alternative was preferred when decision time was unlimited. This change of preference seemed to be the result of the decision makers becoming more influenced by poor scores on the most important attribute when under pressure to reach a quick decision. For example, expensive options were eliminated. Another factor was the increased importance given to the already initially most important attribute in the time-pressured decision. Not surprisingly, under time-stressed decision making, simple decision strategies are used by decision makers.

Russo has shown that choices are influenced strongly by the way in which information is presented.[5] In a study in a supermarket context, he noted that unit prices of similar products are usually displayed singly by the side of a particular product rather than in a grouped display. It follows that the customer's information processing will be influenced by the sequence in which they come across the individual brands as they walk along a supermarket aisle. Russo arranged for unit price information for a range of similar products to be displayed at the end of the aisle and these lists were ordered with the most expensive at the top of the list and the cheapest at the bottom. In his study of real customers, he found that shoppers chose cheaper brands in those supermarkets where he had displayed the listed information.

One implication is that supermarket owners will obtain higher revenues by not displaying such lists. The second, more general implication is that choice can be influenced and changed by changing the way in which information for the decision is obtained.

Making trade-offs

How should choices involving multiple attributes be made? The key focus is on providing a compensatory process where relatively low scores on highly important attributes can, in principle, be compensated for by relatively high scores on less important attributes. For example, in choosing a house, the number of bedrooms, location, style and condition may well need to be balanced against one another, and all these benefits then balanced against cost. Such a compensatory process has been advocated for over two centuries.

In July 1772, Lord Shelburne asked Joseph Priestley to be his librarian. The offer, although both financially and personally appealing, put the scientist in a quandary. On the one hand, Lord Shelburne was as personally attractive as the salary: 'For ability and integrity together, the very first character in this kingdom.' On the other hand, Priestley's current life in Leeds was comfortable and productive and he had not contemplated moving, except perhaps to America. Priestley thought long and hard about the decision and consulted his friend Benjamin Franklin, who suggested a solution to the dilemma by way of 'prudential algebra'. Franklin's advice to Priestley, in a letter dated 19 September 1772, is often cited as the first documented example of a multi-attribued value approach to choice. Franklin advised:

> *When these difficult cases occur, they are chiefly because while we have them under consideration all the reasons pro and*

con are not present to the mind at the same time; but sometimes one set present themselves, and at other times another, the first being out of sight. Hence the purposes or inclinations that alternatively prevail, and the uncertainty that perplexes us. To get over this, my way is, to divide half a sheet of paper by a line into two columns, writing over the one Pro and over the other Con. Then during three or four days consideration I put down under the different heads short hints of the different motives that at different times occur to me for or against the measure.

When I have got them all in one view, I endeavour to estimate their respective weights … and through the weight of reasons … I think I can judge better, and am less likely to make a rash step.[6]

How to make trade-offs

There are five steps to successful compensatory choice:

Step 1

Identify the choice alternatives. In John Bull's candidate selection task, the alternatives are:

- Jack
- Jim
- Jill
- Brian.

Step 2

Identify the attributes that are relevant to the decision problem. For John Bull, these are:

- qualifications
- experience
- personality fit
- references
- intellectual fit
- interview performance.

John felt that the attributes were separable and each one was able to stand alone in relation to each of the other attributes. He didn't feel that he was double counting. He felt that interview performance could encapsulate the candidates' knowledge and interest in potential new employers, and that personality fit could encapsulate the candidate's requisite personal drive and ambition. He felt that each of the six attributes was concrete enough to rate each job candidate against. He didn't feel that he had left any attributes out of consideration.

Step 3

For each alternative, assign scores to measure the performance of the alternative on that attribute. Here the performance is measured on a 0–100 scale, with 0 points assigned to the alternative that scores the worst – of those alternatives under direct consideration – and 100 points assigned to the alternative that scores the best. For John Bull, these are:

	Qualifications	Experience	Personality fit	References	Intellectual fit	Interview performance
Jack	100	0	60	100	70	60
Jim	90	70	100	30	40	0
Jill	70	10	0	0	100	50
Brian	0	100	100	50	20	100

Step 4

Determine a weight for each attribute to reflect how important that attribute is to the decision maker relative to the other attributes. A key point for John Bull to take into account is the range – from the worst scoring alternative to the best scoring alternative – on a single attribute. For example, imagine that you were considering applying the trade-off approach to choosing a small car. You may feel intuitively that miles per gallon (mpg) is a crucial attribute since you have only a small operating budget. But what if the highest and lowest mpg rates were 50 and 47 for the cars that you were considering purchasing? Clearly, the 50-mpg car would be the best and the 47-mpg car would be the worst on the mpg attribute. But notice that the range of mpg is very small, and so will have little impact on your operating budget over a year. It follows that your weighting of mpg as an attribute in your choice should reflect this small and insignificant range. For John Bull, the range over the four candidates on intellectual fit was quite small – all the candidates had the intellect for the job – so he chose to adjust his intuitive weightings to reflect this. By contrast, the range of personality fit was large and significant, so he chose to reflect this in the large weighting for that attribute. One way to check for range effects when weighting attributes is to imagine an alternative – in John Bull's case a candidate – that scores the worst on all of the attributes. Given that you can imagine such a candidate, then which single score would you choose to swing from worst to best? If the score is that of personality fit, then this result would show that the most weight should be allocated to this attribute. Given this swing, what is the next score that you would choose to swing from worst to best? This swing identifies the next most important attribute.

Once this ordering of swings is achieved, more exact weightings are needed. One straightforward way to do this is to distribute 100 points between the attributes. John distributed the points in this way:

Personality fit	30
References	25
Interview performance	15
Qualifications	15
Experience	10
Intellectual fit	5

Step 5

For each alternative, calculate the sum of the weighted scores assigned to that alternative. For John Bull, the weighted scores for Jack were:

Attribute	Score	Weight	Weight × score
Personality fit	60	30	1800
References	100	25	2500
Interview performance	60	15	900
Qualifications	100	15	1500
Experience	0	10	0
Intellectual fit	70	5	350
Total			**7050**

The same computations for Jim's scores on the weighted attributes produced a grand total of 6000. In summary, for each of the four candidates the weighted scores were:

Jack	7050
Jim	6000
Jill	2400
Brian	6850

So in terms of weighted scores, Jack is the best candidate. Such a choice approach is compensatory, in that low scores on highly weighted attributes can be compensated for by high scores on less important attributes. Compensatory choice is more complicated to achieve than choice by elimination, but, as we have argued, the result is a choice of the alternative that overall is the best balanced in terms of trade-offs. Since in everyday life, we don't often use this approach to make choices, then the rigour of adopting a compensatory approach will improve your decision making.

Trade-offs and sensitivity of choice

Sensitivity analysis is a development of the compensatory choice approach. To what extent do changes in weightings and scorings have an impact on the recommended choice? For example, if John's estimate of a 30-point weighting on personality fit were to drop to 20 points, and the weighting on interview performance rose to 25 points, then the weighted scores of each of the four candidates would also change, thus:

Jack	7050
Jim	5000
Jill	2900
Brian	6850

The essence of sensitivity analysis is to explore whether reasonable changes in the relative weightings of the attributes have an impact on the recommended compensatory decision. If they don't, then the decision recommendation is said to be robust. In John Bull's case, the change in weightings above does not alter the weighted scores of the top two candidates, whose total weighted scores remain unchanged in this instance. If small changes in some weightings – or small changes in some scores – change the recommended decision, then this is obviously worth exploring further, since the decision is sensitive to plausible changes in some scores or weightings. Sensitivity analysis is also very useful when a team of managers is charged with making a choice – say of contractors for software development. It may well be that although the managers differ in their weightings of attributes and scoring of the contractors on these attributes, the overall choice recommended by the compensatory approach is common to all.[7]

Overall, then, we don't naturally make choices amongst multi-attributed alternatives using trade-offs in our thought processes. Psychologists have reasoned that the complexity of the trade-offs is too difficult to achieve by mental arithmetic. Since an ability to accomplish such trade-offs is the essence of rational choice, then the five-step procedure is a simple aid to improve on our intuitive choice strategies by making them compensatory.

And the advice for John Bull? Follow the five-step procedure for compensatory choice. Distrust intuition in situations where the alternatives under consideration have multiple attributes of value and cost, since it is likely that intuitive choice will be non-compensatory and thus flawed.

Key messages

This chapter has demonstrated the logic of making choices by a compensatory approach using trade-offs. But this approach cannot be achieved without paper-and-pencil calculations. By contrast, other ways of making such choices – by using elimination, satisficing or focusing solely on what is considered to be the most important attribute – are more characteristic of everyday decision making. This is because these methods are easy to apply and easy to justify to others. But such simplicity in approach will, as we have seen, result in poor-quality decisions.

Good-quality decision making involves identifying the important attributes of a particular choice, scoring the alternatives under consideration on these attributes, and then weighting the relative importance of the attributes. Finally, the alternative with the highest weighted score should be chosen. Such a compensatory choice approach is complicated, but the result is a choice that is the best balanced in terms of well-thought-through trade-offs.

EIGHT

Harnessing the Minds of Managers

Jim Tattle looked around the table. Each of his heads of divisions looked back at him. They were all bright and motivated, but somehow the strategy away-day didn't seem to be working. The idea had been to look into the future: to try and define new products/ services; to move away from the tried and trusted; to re-energise this top management team. We were going through the motions – fair enough – but there was no buzz. Jim had even hired a facilitator to help energise the group. The result was about 50 flip charts stuck to every vertical surface. But what next? Everyone had had their say about what they saw as the issues and potential ways forward for the organisation. Indeed, a few of of the more vocal individuals had engaged in hot debate with one another. But there had been no creative spark – no productive engagement with the issues. Just then, coffee was wheeled in. The meeting adjourned, and each of the divisional heads used their mobile phones to check that nothing had faltered back at the ranch while they were absent.

What was going wrong? How could the situation be improved? Overall, the approach of trying to generate ideas from within the management team is right. Strategy away-days are, in principle, a step in the right direction. Organisations must renew themselves to survive. Success is grounded in the uniqueness of the business offerings. Competencies and ways of doing business that are shared with other organisations will cease to be advantages. Organisations exist in conditions of continuous change – what worked well in the past may be out of date in the future. However, cook-book approaches to developing strategy cannot provide the building blocks for uniqueness, since if an approach has been documented in a business text, then the approach is, in principle, available to business organisations across the world.

Strategy development

Essentially, successful strategy must be invented within the organisation. To my mind, the key resource of the organisation is the heterogeneity of knowledge and the intelligence of its human resources. It follows that the strategic possibilities for the organisation exist in the heads of the participants in the strategic discussion – partly shared and partly individual. The major task for a leader is to harness this intellectual resource. Once harnessed, the likelihood is that there will be recognition that the organisation must change to re-align itself with changes in the business environment.

But strategic adjustment within the organisation is complex. Change is achieved through people: strategy development and successful strategy implementation cannot be separated. Facilitation of group processes and people skills are crucial to harness these intellectual resources in order to generate strategic choices. The process of strategy development will also, if handled correctly, create shared vision and understanding within the management team. After the inevitable bargaining and compromise, a well-thought-out process can also promote group and individual commitment to action and implementation.

All this seems a long way away from the dilemma facing Jim Tattle. Somehow, he has to create the buzz within his management team, and develop shared vision and subsequent commitment. At the moment, the participants seem more concerned with fire-fighting local hot spots within their divisional concerns.

In fact, most management activity is so focused – near-term issues tend to dominate individual managers' agendas. But a focus on fire-fighting to ensure that, say, the production line of a portable CD music player is working efficiently may prove to be ultimately futile with the advent of new technologies such as solid-state MP3 players. Strategic thinking must have a place high on the top-team agenda. The question is, how can this be achieved?

Jim Tattle is part of the way there. Getting ideas on to flip-charts highlights problems and opportunities that individual managers find important. Ideas about strategic direction can be captured in this way. But such data capture is poor at verifying that the meaning and implications of issues – captured as bullet points on a flip chart – are shared among members of the management team. What, then, is the next step for Jim Tattle? Somehow he has to help the team achieve high performance in their strategy development. This outcome can be achieved if an independent facilitator has process tools to activate and stimulate strategic thinking in the top management team.

But facilitation of strategic thinking has potential pitfalls. The individual members of the team will hold diverse viewpoints, some of which may be complementary or contrasting. But some viewpoints may conflict. The outcome of the process is unknown when the process of facilitation begins. It may be that the CEO's view of the direction in which the organisation should be headed is countered strongly by the outcome of the process. The thinking that is activated in the group will be open-ended, and the interaction between individuals will also be, to a large extent, unpredictable. For some CEOs, this uncertainty is threatening. Many individuals view the role of the top manager as setting the direction and determining the strategy. For some CEOs, the process of harnessing the intellectual capability of the management team is thus threatening to their own position in the organisation. So, harnessing intellects takes a special type of leader – one who is comfortable with challenge and is prepared to facilitate and support others when they are the source of ideas for change in the organisational direction. As we shall see, creating a new direction is difficult – but deferring to others' better ideas is more so.

A technique for the facilitation of strategic thinking

The essence of the technique is simple – the ideas of individuals are captured on post-it notes or magnetic shapes that adhere to and yet can be moved over a whiteboard.

The process might start with the facilitator asking each team member to identify three key uncertainties in the business environment that could impact upon the issue of concern – an often-used issue is the survival of the organisation. The facilitator does a round-robin of the group; each key uncertainty is captured in a few words and given a number from a series for subsequent identification. If there are 10 members in the management team, then 30 key uncertainties are identified. Notice that each individual knows that their ideas are being captured. With this method, dominant individuals have no more airtime than others, so evenness of contribution is facilitated. Also, personal attachment to ideas is de-emphasised, and the time sequence of individual contributions does not distort the process. Compare this with a conversation about strategy. Here, vocal individuals may dominate the discussion and points made by some individuals at the start of any discussion may be forgotten as the conversation develops.

The next step is clustering the points to form higher-level groupings. These groupings are formed in an interactive manner as the group of managers gathers around the whiteboard. These clusters can then be named by the group and, as a result of this particular process, for example, key driving forces can be identified to be used in a scenario planning exercise – like that described in Chapter 4. A similar approach can be used to identify the organisation's internal strengths and competencies and, subsequently, derive the business idea that systemically links these – analogous to the one that we derived for the business school in Chapter 4.

The role of the facilitator

Often in such interacting groups, the group process needs helping along. An experienced facilitator will mirror – reflect back, or paraphrase – a contribution from a team member in order to ensure that the rest of the team fully understand the contribution. Experienced facilitators will also use open rather than closed questions, such as 'Do you agree with this?' or 'Are you saying that ...?' In this way, contributions from quieter group members are encouraged.

Other ways of encouraging participation include asking questions such as 'Who hasn't spoken so far?' or 'What is your opinion, Jack?'

Table 4 illustrates the differences between discussions in conventional groups and those in well-facilitated groups.

Table 4 *Facilitated versus conventional group dynamics*

Facilitated groups	Conventional groups
Everyone participates.	Dominant individuals, fast thinkers, and most articulate speakers get more airtime.
People give others time to think and express their opinion.	People interrupt each other to make their own points.
Opposing viewpoints are listened to and evaluated carefully.	Differences of opinion are treated as conflicts that must be resolved one way or the other.
People draw each other out with supportive questions: 'Is this what you mean?'	Questions are often perceived as challenges, as if the person being questioned has to be 'beaten'.
People are able to listen to each other's ideas because they know their own ideas will also be heard.	People have difficulty listening to each other's ideas because they're busy rehearsing what they want to say.
Each group member feels able to speak up on matters of controversy. Everyone knows where everyone stands.	Some group members remain quiet on controversial matters. No-one really knows where everyone stands, or some may think that they do when in fact they don't.
Members can accurately represent each other's points of view – even when they don't agree with them.	People rarely give accurate representations of the opinions and reasoning of those whose opinions are at odds with their own.
Even in the face of opposition, people are encouraged and feel able to stand up for their beliefs.	People with discordant, minority perspectives are commonly discouraged from speaking out.
A problem is not considered solved until everyone who will be affected by the solution understands the reasoning.	A problem is considered solved as soon as the fastest thinkers have reached an answer. Everyone else is then expected to sign up, regardless of whether or not they understand the logic of the decision.

Experienced facilitators realise that disagreement amongst team members is a natural result of different personalities, views and opinions, and that conflicts can be synergistic and lead to major breakthroughs in strategic thinking. However, disagreements must be handled carefully, and the facilitator should not become enmeshed in the content of the conflict and must be sensitive to the feelings of uninvolved group members. Clearly, opposing viewpoints can have validity, and each needs to be treated with respect as an opinion – rather than some viewpoints being dismissed on the basis of an emotional reaction to the speaker.

Lessons from this book

In summary, this book has illustrated pitfalls in strategic choice. In Chapter 1, we saw that strategy can become habitual – tried and trusted success formulas become programmed into organisational life. The success formula of Marks & Spencer and its eventual failure was used to illustrate this. Additionally, the role an individual takes in on organisation can frame the ways that problems and opportunities are viewed. Well-rehearsed and familiar ways of making decisions may become dominant and difficult to change. Even the way a situation is described – for example, emphasising losses or gains in an identical decision – can influence the way we make our choice. Alternative framings of a decision or issue need to be placed on the top-team agenda so that current ways of doing business can be challenged and any framing bias overcome. Frame analysis is one way to achieve this.

But such challenge is often not found in organisations. Decisions once made or strategies once formulated are seldom reversed. Dissenting opinion is often stifled in an emerging consensus. Cohesive groups tend to develop rationalisations for the invulnerability of the groups' decision or strategy. Contingency plans for failure in the preferred course of action are seldom thought through. Groupthink was illustrated in the events leading up to the launch of the space shuttle Challenger and in the management style of Marks & Spencer. Fortunately, the techniques of dialectical inquiry and devil's advocacy provide a structured method for generating alternative viewpoints in top management teams. In a similar way, the method for facilitating top team decision making, outlined at the beginning of this chapter, will surface alternative viewpoints. All three techniques lead to a more critical evaluation of assumptions, and are structured methods for encouraging dissenting opinion. Dissension is useful and adds positively to critical strategic debate. Such debate is needed because management judgement is often overconfident and, commonly, evidence is sought to confirm rather than disconfirm predictions and decisions. Managers have a strong tendency to see an individual forecasting problem as a unique one-off event rather than instances of a broader class of event, but our forecasting ability is poor. Best-guess predictions often turn out to be wrong. We illustrated this with newspaper articles that attempted to predict residential house price movements in the UK.

Scenario planning is a major way of planning for a range of plausible futures that downplays managers' limited ability to make valid best-guess predictions. In this approach, dissenting opinion about the nature of the future is also given airtime – rather than being suppressed by inappropriate cohesion in the top management team, as it strives to reach a consensus. In short, the intellectual resources of an organisation are precious, and heterogeneity should be nurtured and cherished rather than quashed. We illustrated the power of scenario planning with reports of Shell's success. Nevertheless, scenario planning presents challenges to an organisation and its top team. Constructed futures may be unfavourable to the organisation, and current and alternative strategies may be seen to perform poorly against the range of plausible futures. In such instances, the stress of the mismatch is reduced by psychological coping mechanisms. Here, top teams tend to procrastinate, bolster the failing strategy, or pass the responsibility for the decision dilemmas to others. In short, environmental threats to the organisation's survival are not recognised as such. Groupthink processes enhance this myopia. For this reason, we advocate that scenario planning should be a standard technique for organisational renewal, since the value of its ability to increase perceptions of threat and facilitate strategic change may not be recognised by top management.

Additionally, poor outcomes of a decision are, paradoxically, indicative of a good decision process. Many managers act to maximise the minimum pay-off from a decision – such that if the worst comes to the worst, all is not lost. But effective decision making can involve risk taking, which includes the possibility of poor outcomes. By expectation, poor outcomes are a foreseeable part of an excellent decision process. But a blame culture in an organisation discourages calculated risk taking and encourages risk avoidance with its inherent lower expectation of long-term gain. Also, a 'blame culture' encourages irrational escalation of commitment to failing strategies. We used articles describing Taurus, the Millennium Dome and Nick Leeson's activities at Barings Bank to illustrate this.

Many decisions involve complex trade-offs between several attributes. Busy mangers tend to focus on what they see as the key criteria rather than on what are seen as less important criteria, but poor performance of an alternative on an important attribute can be compensated for by good performance on less important attributes. Carefully balanced decision making is rational – Chapter 7 provides a five step method for compensatory choice.

Key learning points are:

- Challenge success formulas.
- Contest the status quo.
- Reframe problems and opportunities.
- Apply frame analysis to surface new framings.
- Disband cohesive groups.
- Confront groupthink.
- Encourage dissenting opinion.
- Recognise overconfidence.
- Search for disconfirming information.
- Challenge hindsight.
- Create and think about plausible futures.
- Search for robust strategies.
- Look for trigger events that indicate the unfolding of favourable and unfavourable scenarios.
- Don't procrastinate.
- Don't shift responsibility.

- Don't bolster failing strategies.
- Accept the stress of decision dilemmas.
- Accept calculated risks.
- Accept that good decision processes can result in poor outcomes.
- Remove a blame culture.
- Require that new decision makers review the need for further allocation of funds to ongoing projects.
- Analyse difficult decisions using conscious trade-offs – avoid non-compensatory choice.
- Resist time pressure in your decision making, otherwise you will tend to make non-compensatory choices.
- Use facilitators to harness the intellectual resource of your organisation.

Above all, remember that the key resource of your organisation is the intellectual capability held in the heads of the individual managers. In many organisations, this resource is largely untapped. Unique competitive advantage lies in harnessing this resource and using it to drive your organisation forward. This book has shown you how to achieve this, and has illustrated what can happen to organisations that don't.

Notes

Chapter 1

1. Luchins, A.S. and Luchins, E.G. (1959) *Rigidity of Behavior*, University of Oregon Press: Eugene, Oregon.

   Sheerer, M. (1963) Problem solving, *Scientific American*, **208**, 118–128.

2. Russo, J.E. and Schoemaker, P.J.H. (1989) *Decision Traps*, Doubleday: New York.

3. Huff, J.O., Huff, A.S. and Thomas, H. (1992) Strategic renewal and the interaction of cumulative stress and inertia, *Strategic Management Journal*, **13**, 55–75.

   Barr, P.S., Strimpert, J.L. and Huff, A.S. (1992) Cognitive change, strategic action and organisational renewal, *Strategic Management Journal*, **13**, 15–36.

   Porac, J.F., Thomas, H. and Baden-Fuller, C. (1989) Competitive groups as cognitive communities: the case of Scottish knitwear manufacturers, *Journal of Management Studies*, **26**, 397–416.

   Miller, D. and Chen, M.-J. (1994) Sources and consequences of competitive inertia: a study of the U.S. airline industry, *Administrative Science Quarterly*, **39**, 1–23.

   See also: Hannan, M.T. and Freeman, J.H. (1984) Structural inertia and organisational change, *American Sociological Review*, **49**, 149–164.

   Miller, D. and Friesen, P. (1980) Momentum and revolution in organisational adaption, *Academy of Management Journal*, **23**, 591–614.

   Johnson, G. (1988) Rethinking incrementalism, *Strategic Management Journal*, **9**, 75–91.

   Hodgkinson, G.P. (1997) Cognitive inertia in a turbulent market: the case of UK residential estate agents, *Journal of Management Studies*. **34**, 921–945.

   Reger, R.K. and Palmer, T.B. (1996) Managerial categorization of competitors: using old maps to navigate new environments, *Organisation Science*. **7**, 22–39.

4. Taken from Tversky, A. and Kahneman, D. (1981) The framing of decisions and the psychology of choice, *Science*, **211**, 453–458.
5. McNeil, B.J., Pauker, S.G., Sox, H.C. and Tversky, A. (1982) On the elicitation of preferences for alternative therapies, *New England Journal of Medicine*, **306**, 1259–1262.
6. Adaption from Russo and Schoemaker's Frame Analysis Worksheet (in note 2, above).

Chapter 2

1. Janis, I.R. (1982) *Groupthink*, 2nd edn, Houghton Mifflin, Boston.

   Esser, J.K. and Lindoerfer, J.S. (1989) Groupthink and the Space Shuttle Challenger Accident: towards a quantitative case analysis, *Journal of Behavioral Decision Making*, **2**, 167–177.

   See also Park, W.W. (1990) A review of research on groupthink, *Journal of Behavioral Decision Making*, **3**, 229–245.
2. See Sandberg, A., Schweiger, C. and Ragan, F. (1986) Group approaches for improving strategic decision making, *Academy of Management Journal*, **29**, 51–71.

Chapter 3

1. Taken from Goodwin, P. and Wright, G. (1988) *Decision Analysis for Management Judgment*, John Wiley & Sons: Chichester.
2. Taken from Einhorn, H.J. (1980) Overconfidence in judgment. In Shweder, R.A. and Fiske, D.W. (eds) *New Directions for Methodology of Social & Behavioral Science,* Josey Bass: San Francisco.
3. Hodgkinson, G. and Wright, G. Confronting strategic inertia in a top management team: learning from failure, *Organisation Studies*, in press.
4. Taken from Evans, J. St. B.T. (1987) Beliefs and expectations as causes of judgmental bias, in Wright, G. and Ayton, P. (eds) *Judgmental Forecasting*, John Wiley & Sons: Chichester.
5. For a review, see Klayman, J. and Ha, U.-W. (1987) Confirmation, disconfirmation, and information in hypothesis testing, *Psychological Review*, **94**, 211–228.
6. Fischhoff, B. (1975) Hindsight and foresight: the effect of outcome knowledge on judgement under uncertainty. *Journal of Experimental Psychology: Human Reception and Performance*, **1**, 288–299.
7. Kahneman, D. and Lovallo, D. (1993) Timid choices and bold forecasts: a cognitive perspective on risk taking, *Management Science*, **39**, 17–31.

Cooper, A., Woo, C. and Dunkelberger, W. (1988) Entrepreneurs perceived chances for success, *Journal of Business Venturing*, **3**, 97–108.

8. Gigerenzer, G. (1994) Why the distinction between single event probabilities and frequencies is important for psychology (and vice versa), in G. Wright and P. Ayton (eds) *Subjective Probability*, John Wiley & Sons: Chichester.

   Sniezek, J. and Buckley, T. (1991) Confidence depends on level of aggregation, *Journal of Behavioral Decision Making*, **4**, 263–272.

9. Taken from Tversky, A. and Kahneman, D. (1982) Judgments of and by representativeness, in D. Kahneman, A. Tversky and P. Slovic, *Judgment under Uncertainty: heuristics and biases*, Cambridge University Press: Cambridge.

Chapter 4

1. Adapted from Irvine, I.W. (1992) Change Management: how a manufacturer is learning to compete in new markets, Strathclyde Graduate Business School MBA dissertation.
2. Van der Heijden, K. (1996) *Scenarios: the art of strategic conversation*, John Wiley & Sons: Chichester.
3. Adapted from Ng, S.M.W. and McConnell, D. (1993) Development of a Coherent European Strategy as Part of a Global Strategy for a Multinational Corporation in Liner Industry, Strathclyde Graduate Business School MBA dissertation.
4. Adapted from Kahane, A. (1992) The Mont Fleur scenarios, *Weekly Mail* and *The Guardian Weekly*.
5. This idea can be traced to the work of Eden, C. and Ackermann, F. (1999) *Strategy Making*, Sage: London.
6. For further reading on scenario planning, see Wack, P. (1985) Scenarios: uncharted waters ahead, *Harvard Business Review*, Sept–Oct, 73–90.

   Wack, P. (1985) Scenarios: shooting the rapids, *Harvard Business Review*, Nov–Dec, 131–142.

   Schoemaker, P.J.H. (1995) Scenario planning: a tool for strategic thinking, *Sloan Management Review*, Winter, 25–40.

   Goodwin, P. and Wright, G. (2001) Enhancing strategy evaluation in scenario planning: A role for decision analysis, *Journal of Management Studies*, **38**, 1–16.

Chapter 5

1. This questionnaire is an adaptation of the Flinders decision making questionnaire reported in Mann, L., Burnett, P., Radford M. and Ford, S. (1997) The Melbourne decision making questionnaire: an instrument for measuring patterns of coping with decisional conflict, *Journal of Behavioral Decision Making*, **10**, 1–19.
2. Janis, I.L. and Mann, L. (1977) *Decision Making: a psychological analysis of conflict*, New York: Free Press.
3. Hodkinson, G. and Wright, G. (1995) 'Confronting strategic inertia in a top management team: learning from failure'. Manuscript available from G. Wright at the Graduate School of Business, University of Strathclyde.
4. Adapted from Wright, G. and Goodwin, P. (1999) Future-focused thinking: combining decision analysis and scenario planning, *Journal of Multi-Criteria Decision Analysis*, **8**, 311–321.

Chapter 6

1. For more detail on decision analysis techniques see Goodwin, P. and Wright, G. (1998) *Decision Analysis for Management Judgment*, John Wiley & Sons: Chichester.
2. Staw, B.M. and Ross, J. (1978) Commitment to a policy decision: a multitheoretical perspective, *Administrative Science Quarterly*, **23**, 40–64.

   Bazerman, M.H., Guiliano, T. and Appelman, A. (1974) Escalation in individual and group decision making, *Organisational Behavior and Human Decision Processes*, **33**, 141–152.

   For a recent review and linkages to organisational decision making, see Drummond, H. (1994) Escalation in organisational decision making: a case of recruiting an incompetent employee, *Journal of Behavioral Decision Making*, **7**, 43–56.

Chapter 7

1. Tversky, A. (1972) Elimination by aspects: a theory of choice, *Psychological Review*, **79**, 281–299.
2. Simon, H.A. (1979) Rational decision making in business organisations, *American Economic Review*, **69**, 493–513.
3. Russo, J.E. and Rosen, L.D. (1975) An eye fixation analysis of multiple-alternative choice, *Memory and Cognition*, **3**, 267–276.

Dahlstrand, U. and Montgomery, H. (1984) Information search and evaluative processes in decision making: a computer based process tracing study, *Acta Psychologica*, **56**, 113–123.

4. Svenson, O. and Edland, A. (1987) Changes of preferences under time pressure, *Scandinavian Journal of Psychology*, **28**, 322–330.
5. Russo, J.E. (1977) The value of unit price information, *Journal of Marketing Research*, **14**, 193–201.
6. Rutt (1831-32) The correspondence of Joseph Priestley. Privately published: London.
7. For more detail on multi-attribute value analysis see Goodwin, P. and Wright, G. (1998) *Decision Analysis for Management Judgment*, John Wiley & Sons: Chichester

Appendix A
Solution to thought problem 3

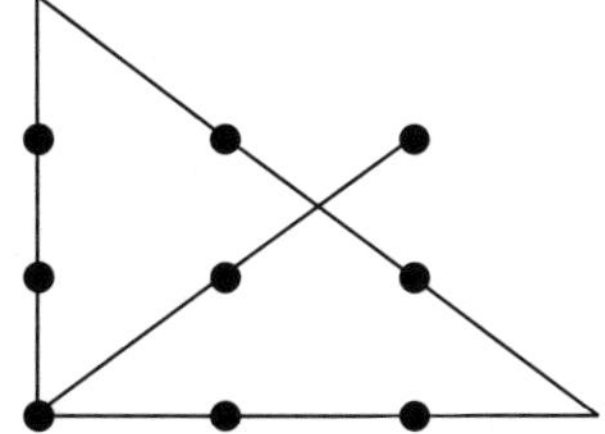

Most people cannot solve the problem because they assume that the lines must stay within the square formed by the dots. But, of course, this assumption is just that, an assumption.

Appendix B

Were you overconfident in your estimates? The true values of the quantities are:

1. 10 118 miles
2. 97 gold medals
3. 839 781 square miles
4. 1938
5. 1876
6. 187 000
7. $105 263 million
8. 1809
9. 14 000 feet
10. 1770 miles

If your 90% was justified, then I would expect nine of your ten ranges to include the true value. If fewer of your ranges achieved this, then this suggests that you were overconfident.

Appendix C

Count the question numbers that you have ticked as follows. The more ticks against each category, then the more your decision making style illustrates:

Defensive avoidance:	3, 8, 13, 20, 22
Bolstering:	1, 11, 14, 18, 25
Procrastination:	7, 10, 15, 23, 26
Shifting responsibility:	4, 6, 16, 19, 24
Vigilance:	2, 5, 9, 12, 17, 21

Index